ACTIVE

SKILLS FOR READING 3

Neil J Anderson

NATIONAL GEOGRAPHIC LEARNING | HEINLE CENGAGE Learning

Australia • Brazil • Japan • Korea • Mexico • Singapore • Spain • United Kingdom • United States

NATIONAL GEOGRAPHIC LEARNING | **HEINLE CENGAGE Learning**

Active Skills for Reading Student Book 3, Third Edition

Neil J Anderson

Publisher, Asia and Global ELT:
  Andrew Robinson

Senior Development Editor:
  Derek Mackrell

Associate Development Editor:
  Sarah Tan

Director of Global Marketing:
  Ian Martin

Academic Marketing Manager:
  Emily Stewart

Marketing Communications Manager:
  Beth Leonard

Director of Content and Media Production:
  Michael Burggren

Associate Content Project Manager:
  Mark Rzeszutek

Manufacturing Manager: Marcia Locke

Manufacturing Planner:
  Mary Beth Hennebury

Composition: PreMediaGlobal

Cover Design: Page2, LLC

Freelance writer: John Murn

Freelance editor: Jenny Wilsen

ISBN-13: 978-1-133-30806-5

ISBN-10: 1-133-30806-6

National Geographic Learning
20 Channel Center Street
Boston, MA 02210
USA

Cengage Learning is a leading provider of customized learning solutions with office locations around the globe, including Singapore, the United Kingdom, Australia, Mexico, Brazil, and Japan.

Cengage Learning products are represented in Canada by Nelson Education, Ltd.

Visit National Geographic Learning online at **ngl.cengage.com**

Visit our corporate website at **www.cengage.com**

Photo credits

FRONT MATTER: Thinkstock: Hemera/Getty Images, Jupiterimages/Getty Images, Jupiterimages/Getty Images, Hemera/Getty Images. **p11:** AARON HUEY/ National Geographic, Angelo Giampiccolo/Shutterstock.com, gh19/Shutterstock.com,VILevi/Shutterstock.com. **p12:** Alfredo Ragazzoni/Shutterstock.com, Comstock/ Thinkstock, sheff/Shutterstock.com, Kraska/Shutterstock.com. **p13:** alexwhite/Shutterstock.com, iofoto/Shutterstock.com. **p14:** Gabriela Insuratelu/Shutterstock.com, iStockphoto/Thinkstock. **p19:** iStockphoto/Thinkstock, PavelSvoboda/Shutterstock.com, STEVE RAYMER/National Geographic. **p20:** TANAYESH TALUKDAR/National Geographic, Jarno Gonzalez Zarraonandia/Shutterstock.com. **p25:** Jason Dewey/Getty Images, Elizabeth Young/Getty Images, JohanJK/Alamy, Africa Media Online/ Alamy. **p27:** Natasha R. Graham/Shutterstock.com, Stuart O'Sullivan/Getty Images, sommthink/Shutterstock.com. **p28:** Anton Oparin/Shutterstock.com. **p33:** s_bukley/ Shutterstock.com, K2 images/Shutterstock.com, illustrart/Shutterstock.com. **p34:** Michael N. Todaro/FilmMagic/Getty Images. **p39:** CHARLES R. KNIGHT/National Geographic. **p41:** JOEL SARTORE/National Geographic, Mirek Srb/Shutterstock.com. **p42:** FRANS LANTING/National Geographic, HEIDI AND HANS-JURGEN KOCH/ National Geographic. **p46:** FRITZ HOFFMANN/National Geographic. **p47:** CHARLES R. KNIGHT/National Geographic, JONATHAN BLAIR/National Geographic. **p48:** KAREN KASMAUSKI/National Geographic. **p53:** RALPH LEE HOPKINS/National Geographic. **p55:** MICHAEL MELFORD/National Geographic, FRANS LANTING/ National Geographic. **p56:** FRANS LANTING/National Geographic. **p59:** Justin Kase zsixz/Alamy, STEVE MCCURRY/National Geographic. **p60:** Janine Wiedel Photolibrary/ Alamy, **p62:** FRANS LANTING/National Geographic. **p63:** JOEL SARTORE/National Geographic, GREG WINSTON/National Geographic, JIM AND JAMIE DUTCHER/National Geographic. **p65:** Wattie Cheung/AFP/Getty Images/Newscom. **p66:** AMY WHITE & AL PETTEWAY/National Geographic, RICH REID/National Geographic. **p67:** Vorobyeva/ Shutterstock.com, Frederic Soltan/Corbis. **p68:** Sweetok/Shutterstock.com. **p73:** Andre Blais/Shutterstock.com, Colin McPherson/Corbis. **p74:** Corey Lowenstein/Landov. **p79:** CARLOS PAILLACAR/National Geographic, SCOTT S. WARREN/National Geographic, Blend Images/Shutterstock.com. **p81:** AJ WILHELM/National Geographic. **p82:** India Images/Alamy Limited, Paula Solloway/Alamy Limited. **p85:** kuleczka/Shutterstock.com. **p87:** Per-Andre Hoffmann/Aurora Photos. **p88:** AP Photo/Wally Santana. **p93:** Dale O'Dell/Alamy, dieKleinert/Alamy.EPA/CORBIS/National Geographic Stock, Alfred Gescheidt/Getty Images. **p94:** NASA Images, Brandon Alms/iStockphoto.com. **p95:** THOMAS MARENT/National Geographic, CH'IEN LEE/National Geographic. **p96:** ROBERT MADDEN/National Geographic, Photos 12/Alamy. **p101:** Sergey Mironov/ Shutterstock.com, Mary Evans Picture Library/ Alamy, Mary Evans Picture Library/ Alamy. **p102:** Robert Red/Shutterstock.com, Shaiith/Shutterstock.com. **p107:** Michael Appleton/NY Daily News via Getty Images. **p109:** AP Photo/Bob Bird. **p111:** AP Photo/Jeff Gentner. **p113:** aPERFECT/Shutterstock.com, Mihai-Bogdan Lazar/Shutterstock.com. **p114:** MIXA/Getty Images, amana images inc./Alamy. **p116:** Jean-Edouard Rozey/Shutterstock.com, MICHAEL & JENNIFER LEWIS/National Geographic. **p117:** Wikipedia, Mary Evans/Science Source/Photo Researchers, Inc. **p121:** zphoto/Shutterstock.com, Dmitry Berkut / Shutterstock.com, Bine/Shutterstock.com. **p126:** Hkannn/Shutterstock.com. **p127:** Tom Wang/Shutterstock.com. **p128:** ROBB KENDRICK/National Geographic. **p133:** JON T. SCHNEEBERGER/National Geographic, SKIP BROWN/National Geographic, Alessio Moiola/Shutterstock.com, GREG DALE/National Geographic, JACOB J. GAYER/National Geographic. **p134:** JON T. SCHNEEBERGER/National Geographic. **p135-6:** NASA/National Geographic. **p140:** Keystone View Co/ National Geographic, MARKA/Alamy. **p141:** AP Photo, Christopher Parypa/Shutterstock.com. **p142:** JAMES L. AMOS/National Geographic. **p147:** wong yu liang/Shutterstock.com, Sergey Momotyuk/Shutterstock.com, paul prescott/Shutterstock.com, wavebreakmedia/Shutterstock. com. **p149:** Pressmaster/Shutterstock.com, Gladskikh Tatiana/Shutterstock.com. **p150:** Emese/Shutterstock.com. **p155:** hartphotography/Shutterstock.com. **p156:** Sergey Nivens/Shutterstock.com. **p162:** rosym/Shutterstock.com, Kzenon /Shutterstock.com. **p163:** David Castillo Dominici/Shutterstock.com, wavebreakmedia/Shutterstock. com. **p167:** Lionel Alvergnas /Shutterstock.com, Algol /Shutterstock.com. **p168:** O. Louis Mazzatenta/National Geographic, Moviestore collection Ltd/Alamy. **p170:** Goodluz /Shutterstock.com, rSnapshotPhotos /Shutterstock.com. **p171:** ruigsantos /Shutterstock.com. **p173:** Lambert/Archive Photos/Getty Images, ClassicStock/Alamy, Sergio Azenha, Alamy, David R. Frazier Photolibrary, Inc./Alamy. **p175:** leungchopan/Shutterstock.com, Jirsak/Shutterstock.com. **p176:** Henri Ensio/Shutterstock.com. **p181:** Zurainy Zain/Shutterstock.com, martan/Shutterstock.com. **p187:** Caimacanul/Shutterstock.com. **p189:** Lightspring/Shutterstock.com, MAGGIE STEBER/National Geographic. **p195:** Zphoto/Shutterstock.com, Andreas G. Karelias/Shutterstock.com. **p201:** Warner Brothers/Everett Collection, Columbia/Everett Collection, Everett Collection, Pictorial Press Ltd/Alamy. **p202:** Warner Bros./Everett Collection. **p203:** WARNER BROS/DC COMICS/The Kobal Collection/Picture Desk, Warner Bros/Everett Collection. **p204:** 20th Century Fox Film Corp/Everett Collection, Warner Bros./ Everett Collection. **p208:** Everett Collection, Warner Bros./ Everett Collection, AF archive/Alamy. **p209:** Renewer/ Shutterstock.com, jmcdermottillo/Shutterstock.com, Jeff Vespa/Getty Images, Dimension Films/ Everett Collection, AF archive/Alamy. **p217:** Sam72/Shutterstock.com, Kamira/ Shutterstock.com, muzsy/Shutterstock.com. **p221:** mikeledray/Shutterstock.com, See Li/Demotix/Corbis. **p222:** See Li/Demotix/Corbis. **p224:** deedl/Shutterstock.com, Pictorial Press Ltd/Alamy, Photos 12/Alamy.

Printed in China
9 10 11 23 22 21

Dedication & Acknowledgments

This book is dedicated to the students and teachers who have used *ACTIVE Skills for Reading* over the past ten years. Since 2002/2003 when the first edition of *ACTIVE Skills for Reading* was published, thousands of students and teachers have used the book. I know that I had no idea that the series would be this popular and that we would reach the stage of publishing a third edition.

The pedagogical framework for this series is as viable today as it has ever been. As students and teachers use each of the elements of *ACTIVE*, stronger reading will result.

My associations with the editorial team in Singapore continue to be some of my greatest professional relationships. I express appreciation to Sean Bermingham, Derek Mackrell, Andrew Robinson, and Sarah Tan for their commitment to excellence in publishing. I also express appreciation to Jenny Wilsen and John Murn for their commitment to helping the third edition be stronger than the two previous editions.

Neil J Anderson

The third edition of *ACTIVE Skills for Reading* maintains the ACTIVE approach developed by reading specialist Professor Neil J Anderson, while introducing several significant improvements.

This new edition now has a full color design, presenting the series' content in an attractive and student-friendly way. Approximately half of the passages have been replaced with new and engaging topics; the rest have been updated. It also has a wide variety of text types including articles, journals, blogs, and interviews, with later levels featuring readings based on content from National Geographic.

Each of the 24 chapters now includes a "Motivational Tips" section from Professor Anderson, reflecting his current research into student motivation and learning. His reading charts have also been updated to more accurately track students' reading fluency and comprehension progress.

ACTIVE Skills for Reading, Third Edition features an Assessment CD-ROM with ExamView® Pro, which has been revised to reflect the needs of learners preparing for standardized tests.

This latest edition of *ACTIVE Skills for Reading* series is designed to further enhance students' progress, helping them to become more confident, independent, and active readers.

Reviewers for this edition ——
Mardelle Azimi; **Jose Carmona** Hillsborough Community College; **Grace Chao** Soochow University; **Mei-Rong Alice Chen** National Taiwan University of Science and Technology; **Irene Dryden; Jennifer Farnell** Greenwich Japanese School; **Kathy Flynn** Glendale Community College; **Sandy Hartmann** University of Houston; **Joselle L. LaGuerre; Margaret V. Layton; Myra M. Medina** Miami Dade College; **Masumi Narita** Tokyo International University; **Margaret Shippey** Miami Dade College; **Satoshi Shiraki; Karen Shock** Savannah College of Art and Design; **Sandrine Ting; Colin S. Ward** Lonestar College; **Virginia West** Texas A&M University; **James B. Wilson; Ming-Nuan Yang** Chang Gung Institute of Technology; **Jakchai Yimngam** Rajamangala University of Technology

Reviewers of the second edition ——————————————————————————————————————
Chiou-lan Chern National Taiwan Normal University; **Cheongsook Chin** English Campus Institute, Inje University; **Yang Hyun** Jung-Ang Girls' High School; **Li Junhe** Beijing No.4 High School; **Tim Knight** Gakushuin Women's College; **Ahmed M. Motala** University of Sharjah; **Gleides Ander Nonato** Colégio Arnaldo and Centro Universitário Newton Paiva; **Ethel Ogane** Tamagawa University; **Seung Ku Park** Sunmoon University; **Shu-chien, Sophia, Pan** College of Liberal Education, Shu-Te University; **Marlene Tavares de Allmeida** Wordshop Escola de Linguas; **Naowarat Tongkam** Silpakorn University; **Nobuo Tsuda** Konan University; **Hasan Hüseyin Zeyrek** Istanbul Kültür University Faculty of Economics and Administrative Sciences

Contents

Vocabulary Learning Tips

Learning new vocabulary is an important part of learning to be a good reader. Remember that the letter **C** in **ACTIVE Skills for Reading** reminds us to **cultivate** vocabulary.

1 *Decide if the word is worth learning now*

As you read, you will find many words you do not know. You will slow your reading fluency if you stop at every new word. For example, you should stop to find out the meaning of a new word if:

    a. you read the same word many times.

    b. the word appears in the heading of a passage, or in the topic sentence of a paragraph—the sentence that gives the main idea of the paragraph.

2 *Record information about new words you decide to learn*

Keep a vocabulary notebook in which you write words you want to remember. Complete the following information for words that you think are important to learn:

New word	healthy
Translation	健康
Part of speech	adjective
Sentence where found	Oliver is well-known for sharing his secrets of cooking healthy food.
My own sentence	I exercise to stay fit and healthy.

3 *Learn words from the same family*

For many important words in English that you will want to learn, the word is part of a word family. As you learn new words, learn words in the family from other parts of speech (nouns, verbs, adjectives, adverbs, etc.).

Noun	happiness
Verb	
Adjective	happy
Adverb	happily

4 *Learn words that go with the key word you are learning*

When we learn new words, it is important to learn what other words are frequently used with them. These are called collocations. Here is an example from a student's notebook.

		long		
take		two-week		next week
go on	a	short	vacation	in Italy
need		summer		with my family
have		school		by myself

5 Create a word web

A word web is a picture that helps you connect words together and helps you increase your vocabulary. Here is a word web for the word *frightened*:

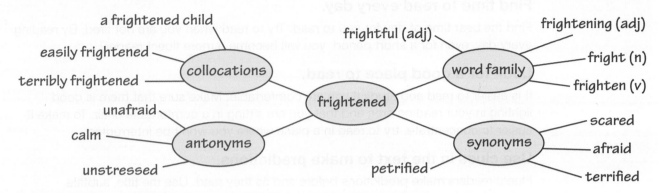

6 Memorize common prefixes, roots, and suffixes

Many English words can be divided into different parts. We call these parts *prefixes*, *roots*, and *suffixes*. A *prefix* comes at the beginning of a word, a *suffix* comes at the end of a word, and the *root* is the main part of the word. In your vocabulary notebook, make a list of prefixes and suffixes as you come across them. On page 175 there is a list of prefixes and suffixes in this book. For example, look at the word *unhappily*.

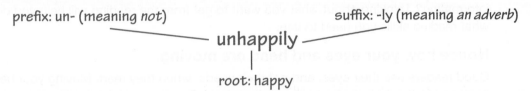

7 Regularly review your vocabulary notebook

You should review the words in your vocabulary notebook very often. The more often you review your list of new words, the sooner you will be able to recognize the words when you see them during reading. Set up a schedule to go over the words you are learning.

8 Make vocabulary flash cards

Flash cards are easy to make, and you can carry them everywhere with you. You can use them to study while you are waiting for the bus, walking to school or work, or eating a meal. You can use the flash cards with your friends to quiz each other. Here is an example of a flash card:

Tips for Fluent Reading

Find time to read every day.

Find the best time of day for you to read. Try to read when you are not tired. By reading every day, even for a short period, you will become a more fluent reader.

Look for a good place to read.

It is easier to read and study if you are comfortable. Make sure that there is good lighting in your reading area and that you are sitting in a comfortable chair. To make it easier to concentrate, try to read in a place where you won't be interrupted.

Use clues in the text to make predictions.

Fluent readers make predictions before and as they read. Use the title, subtitle, pictures, and captions to ask yourself questions about what you are going to read. Find answers to the questions when you read. After reading, think about what you have learned and decide what you need to read next to continue learning.

Establish goals before you read.

Before you read a text, think about the purpose of your reading. For example, do you just want to get a general idea of the passage? Or do you need to find specific information? Thinking about what you want to get from the reading will help you decide what reading skills you need to use.

Notice how your eyes and head are moving.

Good readers use their eyes, and not their heads, when they read. Moving your head back and forth when reading will make you tired. Practice avoiding head movements by placing your elbows on the table and resting your head in your hands. Do you feel movement as you read? If you do, hold your head still as you read. Also, try not to move your eyes back over a text. You should reread part of a text only when you have a specific purpose for rereading, for example, to make a connection between what you read previously and what you are reading now.

Try not to translate.

Translation slows down your reading. Instead of translating new words into your first language, first try to guess the meaning. Use the context (the other words around the new word) and word parts (prefixes, suffixes, and word roots) to help you guess the meaning.

Read in phrases rather than word by word.

Don't point at each word while you read. Practice reading in phrases—groups of words that go together.

Engage your imagination.

Good readers visualize what they are reading. They create a movie in their head of the story they are reading. As you read, try sharing with a partner the kinds of pictures that you create in your mind.

Avoid subvocalization.

Subvocalization means quietly saying the words as you read. You might be whispering the words or just silently saying them in your mind. Your eyes and brain can read much faster than you can speak. If you subvocalize, you can only read as fast as you can say the words. As you read, place your finger on your lips or your throat. Do you feel movement? If so, you are subvocalizing. Practice reading without moving your lips.

Don't worry about understanding every word.

Sometimes, as readers, we think we must understand the meaning of everything that we read. It isn't always necessary to understand every word in a passage in order to understand the meaning of the passage as a whole. Instead of interrupting your reading to find the meaning of a new word, circle the word and come back to it after you have finished reading.

Enjoy your reading.

Your enjoyment of reading will develop over time. Perhaps today you do not like to read in English, but as you read more, you should see a change in your attitude. The more you read in English, the easier it will become. You will find yourself looking forward to reading.

Read as much as you can.

The best tip to follow to become a more fluent reader is to read whenever and wherever you can. Good readers read a lot. They read many different kinds of material: newspapers, magazines, textbooks, websites, and graded readers. To practice this, keep a reading journal. Every day, make a list of the kinds of things you read during the day and how long you read each for. If you want to become a more fluent reader, read more!

Are You an ACTIVE Reader?

Before you use this book to develop your reading skills, think about your reading habits, and your strengths and weaknesses when reading in English. Check the statements that are true for you.

		Start of course	End of course
1	I read something in English every day.	☐	☐
2	I try to read where I'm comfortable and won't be interrupted.	☐	☐
3	I make predictions about what I'm going to read before I start reading.	☐	☐
4	I think about my purpose of reading before I start reading.	☐	☐
5	I keep my head still, and move only my eyes, when I read.	☐	☐
6	I try not to translate words from English to my first language.	☐	☐
7	I read in phrases rather than word by word.	☐	☐
8	I try to picture in my mind what I'm reading.	☐	☐
9	I read silently, without moving my lips.	☐	☐
10	I try to understand the meaning of the passage, and try not to worry about understanding the meaning of every word.	☐	☐
11	I usually enjoy reading in English.	☐	☐
12	I try to read as much as I can, especially outside class.	☐	☐

Follow the tips on pages 8–9. These will help you become a more active reader. At the end of the course, answer this quiz again to see if you have become a more fluent, active reader.

Backpacker

Luxury-seeker

Foodie

Adventurer

Getting Ready

Discuss the following questions with a partner.

1. What is happening in each of the pictures above? How does each label describe the type of traveler?
2. Which kind of traveler are you? Which are you not?
3. How would you pack or prepare for each of these vacations?

CHAPTER 1 Travel and Technology

Before You Read
Making Travel Easier

A Answer the following questions.

1 How has making travel arrangements changed in the last 20 years?
2 Have you ever used the Internet to plan vacations? If so, how?
3 Do you think technology makes vacation planning easier?

B Discuss your answers with a partner.

Reading Skill
Scanning

When we want to find certain information in a text, we don't actually read the entire text, we *scan* it. We move our eyes very quickly across the page to look for the information we need, sometimes using subtitles, numbers, or other key words to help us. Scanning can help you save time looking for information in a text.

A Scan the passage on the pages13–14 for the information below. Check (✓) whether they are used by Geoff, Hannah, and/or Rajeev.

	Geoff	Hannah	Rajeev
Couchsurfing			
Smartphone map			
TripAdvisor			
Airbnb			
Sightseeing apps			
Online forums			
Local hosts			

B Read the entire passage to see if your answers were correct.

C Now read the entire passage again carefully. Then answer the questions on page 15.

Travel and Technology

It wasn't long ago that going on holiday meant visiting or calling a travel agent to book your flights and hotel. Now, technology may be putting these travel agencies out of business. For one, more people are going online to find and compare prices of flights and hotels, and plan their own itineraries,

5 while connecting with other travelers and reading about each others' experiences. The Internet has a wealth of resources so travelers can learn more about their destination, discover local **treasures**, or uncover any **potential** problems they could encounter. Here are three travelers who have not looked back since going online:

Geoff, 37

10

The first thing I do when I'm preparing to travel is to visit traveler-review websites like TripAdvisor. These interactive sites let travelers share their experiences at tourist attractions, restaurants, and hotels. They can give each place a rating, write a review, or discuss them in online forums.

15

Reading the opinions of **genuine** travelers can be much more convincing than any advertisement. On top of that, reviewers often provide tips, like where to find a money changer in a small town, or which is the best room in a hotel. Also, being able to search for attractions by location, price, or quality rating is a big help because the kind of place I'm

20

looking for depends on whether I'm traveling for work or for leisure. When I travel for work, I focus on comfort and location. But when I'm with my wife and three kids, I always try to get the best value for our money. We also love making **personalized** travel plans that focus on our interests, such as food and beautiful beaches.

25

Hanna, 24

I used to accompany my family on package trips with tour guides and expensive accommodation, but traveling like that separates you from the local culture. It's not really my style. When I go traveling by myself, I love to stay with local people, so I use websites like Couchsurfing and Airbnb to find people to stay with. These sites help you connect with someone in your destination city so that you can rent their space or even stay in their **spare** room for free. I find that staying with someone is often more comfortable than staying in a hotel, and it's usually cheaper. Also, by staying with locals, you get to meet new people and can get sightseeing tips about the city you're visiting. I love to experience the culture and not just the tourist attractions. So when I stay with people, I ask them to tell me about cool places they go to, like their favorite cafes, markets, and shops. And by the end of my stay, I've usually made a few friends!

Rajeev, 28

These days, I never leave for a trip without my smartphone. I use apps and the Internet to access maps, airport information, and many other things. I used to take taxis or the subway to get everywhere in a new city. But not only does the cost of these rides **add up**, they're also not a great way to see a city or learn about a new place. With my smartphone, I'm more confident finding my own way around. I always have access to a map, so I do a lot of walking tours. I don't have to worry about getting lost because I can enter my destination into my phone and it will give me directions, and even re-adjusts the **route** if I make a wrong turn. I've even used smartphone apps to tour museums in New York and London. With the right apps and an Internet connection, a smartphone makes **navigating** the city a breeze!

30

35

40

45

50

55

A Choose the correct answers for the following questions.

1 The writer collected these three opinions to _____.
   a convince people that technology is not necessary for travel
   b illustrate the pros and cons of travel-related technology
   c show the different ways people are using technology to improve travel

2 What does the writer mean when he says the three travelers *have not looked back* (line 9)?
   a They only use the best and latest technology when traveling.
   b They now prefer to use technology instead of going to travel agencies.
   c They are thinking back to their experiences using technology while traveling.

3 Why does Geoff like using traveler-review websites?
   a Real travelers often give the most accurate and helpful information.
   b He tries to find the cheapest options for his business trips.
   c The sites help him meet local people in the places he travels to.

4 How do websites like Couchsurfing or Airbnb work?
   a They help you find cheap and comfortable accommodation in hotels.
   b They give you sightseeing tips and information on the local culture.
   c They help you meet local people who are willing to let you stay with them.

5 What does *a smartphone makes navigating the city a breeze* (line 55) mean?
   a It's very easy to get around the city with a smartphone.
   b You get exercise and fresh air doing a walking tour with a smartphone.
   c A smartphone helps you connect to other people for information about a city.

B Answer the following questions using information from the passage.

1 Why does the writer think travel agencies are going out of business?

_____

_____

2 What does Geoff look for when he's traveling for leisure compared to when he's traveling for work?

_____

_____

3 How does Hanna make new friends in the cities she visits?

_____

_____

4 Why doesn't Rajeev like to take taxis or the subway when he's traveling?

_____

_____

5 Which traveler is LEAST likely to use a website like Couchsurfing, and why?

_____

_____

Critical Thinking

C **Discuss the following questions with a partner.**

1 Do you use or know of other travel websites? Describe them.

2 Do you agree with the writer that technology may drive travel agencies out of business? Why, or why not?

Vocabulary Comprehension

Definitions

A **Match the words in the box to the correct definitions. Write a–h. The words are from the passage.**

a treasure	**b** potential	**c** genuine	**d** personalize
e spare	**f** add up	**g** route	**h** navigate

1 _____ the way to get from one place to another

2 _____ extra

3 _____ possible

4 _____ to make one's own; to make for oneself

5 _____ something that is valued highly

6 _____ to increase

7 _____ to plan a path or direction, to find a way

8 _____ real, honest

B **Complete the following sentences with the correct form of the words from A.**

1 When my cousin comes to stay with us he will sleep in the _____ bedroom.

2 Even the art experts found it hard to tell if the painting was _____ or a fake.

3 My football team recently got our uniforms _____ with our names on the back.

4 Many tourists get lost in Beijing's old *hutong* neighborhoods because it can be hard to _____ the small streets.

5 This old photograph of my grandmother is a real _____ of mine.

6 You should find another _____ home. There's a huge traffic jam on the highway.

7 The cost of eating out every night _____ fast, so we started cooking at home to save money.

8 The company has identified _____ customers to test their latest product.

Motivational Tip: A love of reading! Do you enjoy reading? When you think about how much you love to read, it helps you keep a positive attitude, even when you have to read things that are not of your choice (like a textbook).

A With a partner, discuss and write one synonym and antonym for the following words.

Word	Synonym	Antonym
genuine		
comfort		
spare		
frequently		
treasure		

B Write the following words in the correct column. Some words may belong to more than one column.

treasure	potential	value	genuine	add up
navigate	route	convincing	spare	personalized

Noun	Verb	Adjective

C With a partner, discuss how you can group the words in **A** and **B** by topic or category. Fill in the chart below. What other words from the passage can you add to the chart?

Topic/Category	Words
Words to describe expensive things	*treasures, value, quality*

Vocabulary Skill
Organizing Vocabulary

One helpful way to remember new words is to group them into meaningful categories. You can improve your understanding of new words by grouping the new word(s) together with words you already know that have similar meanings and words with opposing meanings. Vocabulary words can also be grouped by their part of speech or even by topic.

Before You Read
Weather and Vacations

A **Answer the following questions.**

1 What kind of weather do you like the best when on vacation?
2 Have your vacation plans ever been spoiled by unpleasant weather?
3 What kind of vacation activities would you do for the following types of weather?

Type of weather	Activities
snowy	
rainy	
very hot	
cool and breezy	

B **Discuss your answers with a partner.**

Reading Skill
Predicting

Before reading, think about what you are going to read by looking at the title and any subheadings, and examining the images. While reading, you should also think about what comes next. This helps you understand the passage better.

A **Look at the title, pictures, and accompanying captions in the passage on the pages 19–20. Then answer the following questions.**

1 Who is probably interested in "selling India's rainy season"?
   a Indian companies that sell water to neighboring countries
   b tour operators who want to convince tourists to visit India during the rainy season
   c Indian weather scientists who are researching ways of preventing the rainy season

2 Which Indian industry does the rainy season probably hurt the most?
   a the agricultural industry
   b the fishing industry
   c the tourism industry

3 What is a "monsoon palace"?
   a a place built during the monsoon season
   b a place built to help people appreciate the beauty of monsoons
   c a place used for traditional ceremonies during the monsoon season

B **Skim the article to see whether your predictions in A were correct.**

C **Now read the entire passage carefully. Then answer the questions on page 21.**

Selling India's Rainy Season

In most parts of the world, storm clouds would be greeted with a frown. But in India, it's said that when the monsoon rains come, a billion people smile. Monsoon season, also known as the rainy
5 season, is closely tied to India's economy. The **abundant** rains bring life to India's farmland, which provides hundreds of millions of jobs to farm workers and helps feed its **vast** population.

Women pick tea leaves in Darjeeling, India, during the monsoon.

While monsoon season is traditionally a joyful
10 and important time for Indian agriculture, it affects the tourism industry in a very different way. During this time, the number of travelers to India can drop by half. Understandably, very few tourists want to spend their holiday in the rain. But there has been a government push over the last few years to **convince** them otherwise: that India's rain is to be celebrated and not 15 **shunned**. "Watching the rains is one of the best sightseeing options I can imagine," says journalist Somini Sengupta, a Calcutta native.

During the monsoon heavy rains happen daily.

Various states have risen to the challenge. Goa (a popular holiday destination near Mumbai) 20 and Kerala in the south have begun offering "monsoon packages." They say the monsoon brings other benefits besides lower off-season

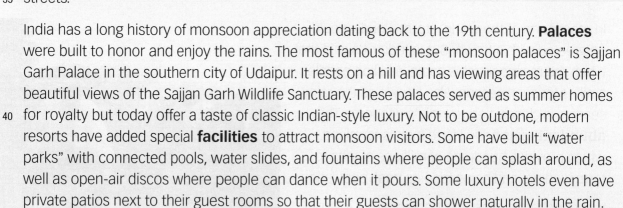
celebrating Rath Yatra in Kolkata

prices. For one, the rain brings with it **lush**, green
25 landscapes. "Goa has beautiful islands, waterfalls,
lakes, dams, and wildlife **sanctuaries** that can be
enjoyed during the monsoons," says Elvis Gomes,
former director of the state's tourism department.

Some of the country's biggest festivals are
30 also held either at the beginning or end of the
monsoon season. For example, Onam festival, held in Kerala in August or September, is a
ten-day-long celebration of the rich harvest, where people eat, sing, dance, and watch the
famous boat races. In the city of Puri on the eastern coast, the Rath Yatra festival features
colorful parades every evening for 21 days, where statues of deities are carried through the
35 streets.

India has a long history of monsoon appreciation dating back to the 19th century. **Palaces**
were built to honor and enjoy the rains. The most famous of these "monsoon palaces" is Sajjan
Garh Palace in the southern city of Udaipur. It rests on a hill and has viewing areas that offer
beautiful views of the Sajjan Garh Wildlife Sanctuary. These palaces served as summer homes
40 for royalty but today offer a taste of classic Indian-style luxury. Not to be outdone, modern
resorts have added special **facilities** to attract monsoon visitors. Some have built "water
parks" with connected pools, water slides, and fountains where people can splash around, as
well as open-air discos where people can dance when it pours. Some luxury hotels even have
private patios next to their guest rooms so that their guests can shower naturally in the rain.

45 Travel writer Alexander Frater spent one whole
monsoon season following the rains up both the
east and west coasts of India. In his book *Chasing
the Monsoon*, he describes the unique energy and
traditions surrounding the monsoons in different
50 regions and cities. Frater noticed that many people
travel to western India during the monsoons seeking
physical and spiritual healing. He quotes a local from
Mumbai who describes the monsoon as a metaphor
for cleansing and rebirth. "The wind drops, it gets very
55 dark, there is terrific thunder and lightning... Suddenly,

a monsoon palace in Udaipur

the air is very cool and perfumed with flowers. It is a time of rejoicing. And renewal."

Many visitors go to India simply to share in this joyous season. As one Kerala promoter says, "You
can feel the magic. The washed streets and fresh leaves seem to smile with you."

A Choose the correct answers for the following questions.

1 The writer's point of view seems to indicate that he or she _____ .
  a works for the Indian government
  b doesn't believe the tourist trade can grow in the rainy season
  c thinks that the rainy season in India is a great travel opportunity

2 Who does *a billion people* refer to on line 3?
  a the population of India
  b the farm workers in India
  c people in countries affected by the monsoon

3 Sajjan Garh Palace is now a _____ .
  a summer home for royalty
  b luxury hotel for monsoon visitors
  c wildlife sanctuary

4 Which is NOT true about Alexander Frater's book?
  a He writes about living in Mumbai for the whole monsoon.
  b He discusses how people visit India to be "healed" by monsoons.
  c He speaks to people in India about their views on the monsoon.

5 The phrase *washed streets and fresh leaves* (line 58) refers to the monsoon as a _____ .
  a cleansing and renewing force
  b blessing for farmland and farm workers
  c time for honor and tradition

B Read the following sentences. Check (✔) whether they are true (T) or false (F).

		T	F
1	The number of tourists to India drops significantly during the monsoon.		
2	The government is trying to increase tourist numbers during the monsoon.		
3	Visiting India during the rainy season is more expensive than other times of the year.		
4	Most festivals are held before the monsoon begins.		
5	The Rath Yatra festival is famous for its boat races.		
6	Many hotels have open areas for guests to enjoy the rain.		

C Discuss the following questions with a partner.

Critical Thinking

1 Would you visit India or other countries during the monsoon? Why, or why not?

2 Can you think of other places where a weak point (like a monsoon) could become a selling point? How would you go about advertising the place?

Vocabulary Comprehension

Odd Word Out

A (Circle) the word or phrase that does not belong in each group. The words in blue are from the reading.

1	persuade	convince	lie	convert
2	shun	interest	lure	attract
3	dusty	dry	dead	lush
4	equipment	features	foodstuff	facilities
5	lacking	abundant	plentiful	sufficient
6	huge	fortunate	tremendous	vast
7	parade	procession	palace	party
8	sanctuary	shelter	safe place	storage

B Complete the following sentences using the words in blue from A. You might have to change the form of the word.

1 La Zisa is a(n) _____ in Italy that was turned into a museum of Arab culture.

2 The island is a(n) _____ for animals because there are very few people living there.

3 Fresh mangoes are _____ in Malaysia in the summer.

4 The salesman _____ me to buy extra equipment to go with my new laptop.

5 The Sahara desert is a(n) _____ area of sand in northern Africa.

6 People started to _____ him because he constantly told lies.

7 Subtropical islands are always _____ and green because of their rainy climates.

8 The hotel I booked has very basic _____; it only has a bed, shower, and wardrobe.

Motivational Tip: Set high expectations! You can do better. Why are you studying English? Why is reading an important part of learning English? In five years time what do you hope to be doing in English? As you respond to these questions, you can set higher expectations for yourself.

A **Match the following words with the correct definitions. Write a–h.**

a offbeat	b off-key	c off-balance	d off-line
e off-limits	f off-road	g offshore	h offscreen

1 _____ not on the correct musical note
2 _____ unusual
3 _____ in a place without any proper streets
4 _____ disconnected from a system, e.g. the Internet
5 _____ not to be entered or used
6 _____ uneven or unsteady
7 _____ not shown in movies or on TV; away from the camera
8 _____ away from land; out in the ocean

B **Complete the following sentences using the correct form of the words from A.**

1 My brother has taken a lot of singing lessons, but he still sings _____ .
2 The army base is _____ to everyone except military personnel.
3 Although he seems arrogant in his movies, the actor is very shy and polite _____ .
4 Having exhausted supplies on land, many companies now drill for oil _____ .
5 The boat was _____ because it was overloaded on one side.
6 I love searching furniture shops for unique pieces with _____ designs.
7 I need to get into the office network, but my computer is still _____ .
8 In order to drive _____ , you need to have a four-wheel-drive vehicle.

C **Can you think of other words that have the prefix *off-*? With a partner, think of three words and come up with example sentences for each of them.**

Vocabulary Skill
The Prefix *off-*

In this chapter, you learned the noun *off-season* meaning *a time of reduced activity*. This word is formed by adding the prefix *off-* to the noun *season*. The prefix *off-* can mean *away from*, *out of*, or *not on*.

Real Life Skill
Planning a Trip Online

It has never been a better time to be a traveler. The Internet and mobile technology continue to improve and offer convenient and helpful new ways to navigate the world. Using Internet, we are able to access a wealth of information and options to help us with our travels.

A **Think of a vacation destination you would like to visit and complete the following chart.**

Destination	Hawaii
Transportation	airplane, cruise ship
Accommodation	luxury resort
Activities	surfing, cycling, swimming
Other information	made up of 18 islands
Travel tip	Drink coconut water—it's refreshing and nutritious!

B **Next, search for transportation, accommodation, three activities you want to do there, and other information for your destination on the Internet. Complete the following chart.**

	Search words	Company	Price
Transportation			
Accommodation			
Activity 1			
Activity 2			
Activity 3			
Other information			

C **Share the information you found with some of your classmates. Do a survey and find out whose travel plan is the most popular.**

What do you think?

1 If you were to create a travel app or website, what would it help people do?
2 What are some of the ways that tourism is promoted in your country?
3 With so many options on the Internet, do you think making vacation plans could actually be harder than before? Why, or why not?

Getting Ready

Discuss the following questions with a partner.

1 What do you understand by the words *fashion*, *style*, or *trend*? Name a person who you think is fashionable.

2 Are you interested in fashion? Why, or why not?

3 Do you think fashion is different in different countries? If so, give some examples.

CHAPTER 1 The Color of Fashion

Before You Read
The Stylemakers

A Who do you think has the most influence on fashion trends? Rank the following from 1–6 (1 = most influential).

_____ designers
_____ clothing brands
_____ celebrities
_____ textile manufacturers (companies who make the fabrics)
_____ consumers
_____ the media (e.g. magazines)

B Discuss your answers with a partner. Give reasons for how you ranked them.

Reading Skill
Skimming for the Main Idea

Skimming is one way to look for the main ideas in a reading. When we skim, we read over parts of the text very quickly, and focus on the first and last paragraphs, and the first sentence of the other paragraphs. We don't need to read every word or look up words we don't understand; we just need to get a general idea of what something is about.

A Skim the passage on the pages 27–28 quickly, then complete the following sentence.

This passage is mainly about _____ .
a companies and organizations that predict future color trends for fashion
b what fashion is and the types of styles and colors that have been influential in recent decades
c how colors influence the way we feel and what clothes we choose to wear

B Discuss your answer with a partner. Explain why you chose it, including any evidence you found when skimming the passage.

C Read the entire passage carefully. Then answer the questions on page 29.

Motivational Tip: Expect success! As you begin this chapter, what do you expect to achieve? Do you expect to improve your reading fluency? Do you expect to increase your vocabulary? When you identify what you want to achieve and then work hard to achieve it, there is a greater chance of success. The challenge is to set a reasonable goal for yourself and expect success.

The Color of Fashion

How do fashion trends begin? Some people assume fashion ideas come straight from designers or from large companies like LVMH (owner of luxury brands like Louis Vuitton). Others believe trends are born on the streets in the form of fashionable individuals. In fact, these designers and well-dressed people, whether they know it or not, are partly influenced by an association that is little-known outside the fashion industry—the Color Marketing Group (CMG).

The sole responsibility of CMG is to decide the "hot" colors for the future. This global association is made up of more than 1,100 contributors who research and predict color trends. The **data** developed by CMG is so influential that it affects not only fashion. Industries like design and architecture or car manufacturers are also involved, as they need to know what the "in" colors are for their products, like wall paint and new cars. Stylist and color expert Kate Smith says that she thinks of CMG as "an invaluable resource when it comes to understanding the direction for design and color for years to come."

CMG's members are always collecting data, information, and samples that will help inform them about future trends. Participating designers consider many aspects of culture when **surveying** color trends, such as movies, music, travel, politics, and the economy. Members of CMG then meet for conferences to **compile** their findings into a report that designers can use as a guide for future seasons' fashion. These reports are used by textile manufacturers, where designers and artists create fabrics and materials that feature the predicted tones. Fashion designers then attend fabric **conventions** to consider the direction they will take with their designs in the upcoming seasons.

CMG is not the only group of its kind, however, and
other color analysts have come to different conclusions
about which colors will be popular in coming years.
In 2012, CMG declared *Boyz-N-Berry*, a bold purple,
to be its "Color of the Year." In contrast, CMG's main
competitor Pantone selected *Tangerine Tango* as its
top color for 2012. A strong red-orange color, Tangerine
Tango was chosen for its energy and strength at a
time when the economy was down, and many people
wanted to cheer up and feel more **optimistic**. "There's
the element of encouragement with orange," said
Leatrice Eiseman, executive director of the Pantone
Color Institute. "It's building on the ideas of courage and
action, that we want to move on to better things."

Boyz-N-Berry walls

Tangerine Tango on the runway

Of course, color
forecasts are not
always perfect. As
the great difference between Boyz-N-Berry
and Tangerine Tango suggests, predicting color
and fashion trends may be more of an art than
a science. Designers may have advice and
direction from organizations that study color,
but they still need to use their own **intuition**
when deciding which advice to follow. In the
end, consumer purchases dictate the trends
that will **stick**, and it's hard to predict how
people will act two years in the future.

Fashion blogger Peter Lappin has pointed to
some surveys that claim U.S. fashion retailers
lose as much as $200 billion dollars a year
because of sales forecast errors. This problem
could result from a number of factors: perhaps designers focused on the wrong
trends or there wasn't enough promotion of the trend. Maybe retailers made
bad decisions with regard to the trends and styles they were presented with.
As Lappin admits, "Nobody knows for sure what's going to happen tomorrow,
whether it's in economics, politics, or fashion." But next time you notice an
abundance of a certain color on the catwalk or on the streets, you'll know it's
down to decisions made years in advance by organizations like CMG.

A **Choose the correct answers for the following questions.**

1   Which statement is true about color trend predictions?
   a   It is usually done by large companies like LVMH.
   b   It has a strong influence even outside fashion.
   c   The companies that specialize in it are very well known.
2   CMG contributors collect color trend data by _____ .
   a   observing different aspects of culture
   b   reading reports by fashion bloggers
   c   attending fabric conventions
3   Tangerine Tango was selected by Pantone because it is _____ .
   a   vibrant and cheerful
   b   calm and relaxing
   c   deep and mysterious
4   Which does NOT prove that color forecasting is an art, not a science?
   a   The big color organizations selected very different colors for 2012.
   b   U.S. fashion retailers sometimes lose money due to forecast errors.
   c   Designers follow the advice they get from color organizations.
5   What is the main idea of the last paragraph?
   a   In the end it's all down to decisions made by retailers and designers.
   b   There are many reasons for why color or trend forecasts go wrong
   c   Color forecasters may not always get it right, but the results are clear when they do.

B **Read the following sentences. Check (✓) whether they are true (T) or false (F).**

		T	F
1	CMG is involved in many things outside of just predicting color trends.		
2	Design and architecture firms use CMG data.		
3	Textile manufacturers create a fashion report that members of CMG use for forecasting.		
4	Fabric conventions are attended by consumers to see the latest color and fashion trends.		
5	Boyz-N-Berry was Pantone's "Color of the Year" in 2012.		
6	Peter Lappin writes about fashion on the Internet.		

C **Discuss the following questions with a partner.**

Critical Thinking

1   Why do you think color is so important to fashion?
2   Do you believe that color influences one's mood or emotions? Give a few examples.

Vocabulary Comprehension

Odd Word Out

A (Circle) the word or phrase that does not belong in each group. The words in blue are from the passage.

1	information	facts	lies	data
2	analyze	distribute	survey	assess
3	stick	remain	stay	depart
4	instinct	intuition	insight	indecision
5	trade	gather	compile	collect
6	match	convention	competition	game
7	optimistic	negative	doubting	pessimistic
8	forecast	predict	remind	anticipate

B Complete the following sentences with the words in blue from **A**. You might have to change the form of the word.

1 The weather _____ isn't very reliable in spring because the weather is so unpredictable then.

2 It's been hard staying _____ after searching for a job for so long with no success.

3 This disease is so rare that it has been difficult for scientists to collect enough _____ to really understand it.

4 We gave George a nickname, but it won't _____ unless everyone uses it.

5 We take our new products to display at a big industry _____ in Paris every year.

6 He does not like to take risks and will always _____ the situation carefully before acting.

7 She has great _____ when it comes to assessing people. She can tell from meeting a person once whether they are trustworthy or not.

8 I am _____ all my best stories and essays to put into my writing portfolio.

A Write the part of speech and a simple definition for the following words. Use your dictionary to help you. Then share your ideas with a partner.

Word	Part of Speech	Definition
dictate		
dictator		
diction		
dictionary		
contradict		
indicate		
predict		
verdict		

Vocabulary Skill
The Root Word *dic/dict*

In this chapter you read the verb *dictate*, meaning to *tell* or *command*. This word is made by combining the root word *dict*, meaning to *say, tell,* or *speak*, with the verb suffix *-ate*. *Dict*, sometimes also written *dic*, is combined with other root words, prefixes, and suffixes to form many words in English.

B Complete the following sentences using the words from **A**. You might have to change the form of the word.

1 After ten years in power, the cruel _____ was finally overthrown.
2 At the end of the court trial, the jury announced its _____ and found the defendant guilty.
3 Can I borrow your _____ for a minute? I need to look up a word.
4 Financial experts _____ that the economy will improve in the second quarter of next year.
5 The fact that Sally never bothers to call Jacob back already _____ a lack of interest in him.
6 He's very argumentative and always feels the need to _____ everything I say.
7 She would make a great news presenter—she speaks clearly and has good _____ .
8 I enjoy my freedom and don't like other people to _____ to me what I can or can't do.

CHAPTER 2 Reality TV: Good or Bad for Fashion?

Before You Read
Reality Television

A **Answer the following questions.**

1 What is reality TV? Which are your favorite reality TV shows?
2 Why is reality TV popular? What makes it so interesting or entertaining?
3 How could fashion design become the focus of a reality show?

B **Discuss your answers with a partner.**

Reading Skill
Identifying Main and Supporting Ideas

Supporting ideas are used to explain or give more information about the main idea of the paragraph. They tend to follow the main idea, which usually appears in the first or second sentence of each paragraph. Different types of supporting ideas include examples, facts, statistics, reasons, etc.

A **Skim paragraph 2 of the article on the next page, then read the following sentences. Identify whether each sentence is a main (M) or supporting idea (S).**

1 _____ Fans follow each episode and even create blogs and write in online forums about the show.
2 _____ More and more students pursue studies in fashion and design, and these departments in universities are growing ever larger.
3 _____ Fashion reality shows have become very popular among a wide audience.

B **Now skim paragraphs 3, 4, and 5 of the article, then read the following sentences. Write the missing main or supporting idea for each paragraph.**

Paragraph 3
Main idea: Fashion reality shows may lead people to think achieving success in the fashion industry is easy.
Supporting idea: _____

Paragraph 4
Main idea: Brands are cautious about working with fashion reality shows and their contestants.
Supporting idea: _____

Paragraph 5
Main idea: _____
Supporting idea: People like fashion legend Calvin Klein do not respect these reality TV shows.

C **Read the entire passage carefully. Then answer the questions on page 35.**

Reality TV: Good or Bad for Fashion?

1 "That's fierce!"

Does that quote make you think of designer Christian Siriano? Siriano, who made the word "fierce" a well-known phrase, has become one of the most successful
5 stars of reality television since winning the fashion contest show *Project Runway* in 2008. However, he is one of very few designers to find real success after appearing on a fashion reality show. With so few success stories to speak of, many people are wondering
10 if these shows are actually helping designers' careers. What's more, many fashion professionals question if the shows are a good thing for the industry.

Christian Siriano won the fourth season of *Project Runway* in the U.S.

2 Fashion reality shows have become very popular among a wide audience.
15 Some shows—such as *Project Runway* or *The Fashion Show*—have been running for several seasons, and fans follow each **episode** and even create fan blogs and write in online forums about the show. Supporters of these shows say they
20 see how professionals work, from sketching ideas to choosing fabric to fitting and accessorizing models. These shows are like a backstage pass to a runway show. Jennifer Minnitti, chairwoman of the department of fashion at the Pratt Institute, agrees
25 that such reality shows have stimulated interest in fashion. As a result of this increased popularity, more and more students **pursue** studies in fashion and design, and these departments in universities are growing ever larger.

3
30 While inspiring students is a good thing, Minnitti points out that some students might be **misled** by fashion reality shows. "You get a lot of students who just want to participate in this program because they want to be on TV, or be a celebrity," says Minnitti. "This is a *tough* business." Minnitti's concern is that these shows make the fashion industry look **glamorous** without giving
35 a true picture of the amount of work involved. Fashion consultant Fern Mallis

agrees. She says that reality shows give people the idea that it can be easy to find fashion success and create their own brand; both extremely rare and difficult things to do. While

40 many contestants from these shows do find work in the fashion industry—as designers for clothing brands, costume designers, etc.— most do not achieve the level of fame or prestige they are seeking.

4 45 The management at clothing brands also seem **cautious** about working with the shows and their former contestants. Brands such as H&M, Macy's, and Saks Fifth Avenue have sponsored TV fashion shows and have offered representatives from their companies as judges. But very few brands have been willing to put their name alongside that of a fashion reality show contestant. This,

50 you might argue, says a lot about the amount of faith companies have in the winners of TV fashion shows. Brand managers know that **collaborating** with a designer or a celebrity can add a new look to their products, make the brand more appealing to consumers, and sell a lot of clothes. But putting out a new clothing

55 line is risky, as it takes a lot of money to produce and promote. This is why brands prefer to work with established designers, like Marc Jacobs, or celebrities, such as Jessica Simpson, who can draw their fans to the brand.

5 60 Major brands have shown that so far they don't believe in the star power of reality show contestants. Fashion legend Calvin Klein is among those in the industry who openly do not respect reality fashion shows, and his comments might explain why brand managers **hesitate**

65 to work with unknown designers. "To really have success and to really make it you need staying power. That's not an accident. These designers work at it all the time, they never stop," says Klein. "A TV show about fashion? That's a **momentary** thing."

Asian-American designer Jason Wu had a successful partnership with Target department store.

A **Choose the correct answers for the following questions.**

1 The purpose of this article is to _____.
   a introduce people to fashion reality shows and its contestants
   b give advice on how to achieve success in the fashion industry
   c discuss if fashion reality shows are beneficial to the industry

2 What does the sentence *These shows are like a backstage pass to a runway show* (line 24) mean?
   a The viewer can see what goes on behind the scenes of a show.
   b The viewer is able to watch runway shows without having to be there.
   c The viewer can pause or rewind the show to view details of the clothes.

3 Which statement is NOT true about fashion reality show contestants?
   a Many of them leave the fashion industry.
   b Very few of them end up like Christian Siriano.
   c Many join these shows so they can appear on TV and be famous.

4 Which brand has probably not worked with a fashion reality show?
   a H&M
   b Saks Fifth Avenue
   c Calvin Klein

5 What does Calvin Klein mean by the phrase "staying power" in line 66?
   a Designers need to stay in one company for some time.
   b Designers need to have the determination to succeed.
   c Designers need to stay away from reality TV shows.

B **The writer describes both positive and negative aspects of fashion reality shows. List at least two pros and two cons in the table below.**

Pros	Cons
	Not many contestants on the shows become successful afterward.

Critical Thinking

C **Discuss the following questions with a partner.**

1 Why do you think people find fashion reality TV shows so inspiring?
2 Do you know of any fashion collaborations between brands and celebrities? Are they successful? Why, or why not?

Vocabulary Comprehension
Words in Context

A **Choose the best answer. The words in blue are from the passage.**

1 Many people are misled by what he says because he tells _____.
   a the truth   b lies

2 Collaboration enables people to work _____.
   a together   b independently

3 The pain is momentary; it'll _____.
   a be over soon   b just get worse

4 Someone who is very cautious doesn't like to _____.
   a relax   b take risks

5 If you hesitate, that dress you like might _____.
   a sell out   b be restocked

6 A TV show with episodes has many _____.
   a parts   b languages

7 Something that is glamorous is usually _____.
   a boring   b exciting

8 I decided to pursue photography as a career because _____.
   a I find it interesting   b it took too much of my time

B **Answer the following questions, then discuss your answers with a partner. The words in blue are from the passage.**

1 What do you think is the ideal length of a TV show episode?
2 Can you name any collaborations between famous musicians?
3 Can you name any occupations that are considered glamorous?
4 Do you think it's good to be cautious? Why, or why not?
5 What does the saying "He who hesitates is lost" mean?
6 Why do you think people say fame is momentary?
7 What kind of career would you like to pursue in the future?
8 Can you give an example of a misleading advertisement? How did it mislead you?

Motivational Tip: Are you a risk-taker? Mistakes are a natural part of the learning process. Are you afraid of making a mistake? Don't be! Think of ways in this unit that you can take a safe risk. Your classroom is the safest place in the world to study English and to make mistakes. If you take a risk and make a mistake, it's okay. What can you learn from making mistakes that will help you improve your reading?

A Read the following paragraph. Discuss with a partner what the words in bold mean.

> Mr. Allen,
>
> I'm writing to complain about the services provided by Fiesta Tours for Woodville High's recent field trip to Mexico. While the children found it an educational experience, it was let down by serious **mismanagement** on your company's part.
>
> For one thing, the hotel was **misinformed** of our arrival time, so we had to wait until 6 PM to check in. We then discovered that our coach driver could not understand English, which led to many problems. For example, in a **misguided** attempt to find us a good place to eat, he drove us to the next town without realizing that we had already made dining arrangements. When we got to the correct restaurant, there was another **misunderstanding**. The restaurant had the **misconception** that, because we were from the U.S., we did not want any spices in our food. Even though the food was tasteless, the children ate it because they were so hungry. Finally, it appears you **miscalculated** the bill for your services—we rented the tour bus for five days, not six. The name of our school is also **misspelled** on the invoice.
>
> Regards,
>
> Ms. Harris

Vocabulary Skill
The Prefix *mis-*

In this chapter, you learned the word *misled*. This word is formed by adding the prefix *mis-* to the verb *led* or *lead*. The prefix *mis-* has a negative meaning and can mean *wrong* or *ill*, or it can simply be used to make the word an antonym (e.g. *mistrust*). It can be added to various parts of speech.

B Complete the following sentences using the *mis-* words in bold from **A**. You might have to change the form of the word.

1 I _____ the amount of money I'd need on vacation, so I had to borrow from my friend.
2 He tries to help out as much as he can, although some of his efforts are somewhat _____.
3 People have this _____ that penguins are only found in icy regions, when in fact some breeds of penguins prefer warm climates.
4 The word *weird* is very commonly _____.
5 She was _____ about where to meet and ended up in a completely different place.
6 The instructions are clearly written so as to avoid any _____.
7 The project was severely _____ and had to be abandoned.

C Choose three *mis-* words and come up with a sentence for each of them.

Real Life Skill
Understanding Clothing Sizes

Countries all over the world have different ways of measuring clothing and shoe sizes. If you plan to visit another country, or are interested in shopping online for yourself or others, becoming familiar with some international clothing sizes can help you to make the right choices.

A Study the charts below. Which measurements are commonly used in your country?

Women's Dresses/Blouses/Sweaters				
	U.S.	U.K.	Europe	Japan
XS	4	8	36	5
S	6	10	38-40	7
M	8	12	42-44	9
L	10	14	46-48	11
XL	12	16	50+	13

Men's Shirt Collar		
U.S./U.K.	Europe	Japan
14	36	36
14.5	37	37
15	38	38
15.5	39	39
16	40	40
16.5	41	42

Women's Shoes			
U.S.	U.K.	Europe	Japan
4	3	36	21.5
5	4	37	22.5
6	5	38	23.5
7	6	39	24.5
8	7	40	25.5

Men's Shoes			
U.S.	U.K.	Europe	Japan
7	6	40	24.5
8	7	41	25.5
9	8	42	26.5
10	9	43	27.5
11	10	44	28.5

B Refer to the charts in **A** to help the following people choose clothes in the right sizes.

1 Kentaro is shopping for clothes in London. He is a Japanese shirt size 37 and shoe size 25.5.
   Shirt: _____   Shoes: _____

2 Birgit is in New York buying presents for her sister who is a European blouse size 42 and shoe size 40.
   Blouse: _____   Shoes: _____

3 Simon has just moved to Tokyo and needs to buy work clothes. He is a U.K. shirt size 15.5 and shoe size 9.
   Shirt: _____   Shoes: _____

4 Anna is shopping on a French website. She is a U.S. dress size 12 and shoe size 7.
   Dress: _____   Shoes: _____

What do you think?

1 People say fashion tends to go in circles, meaning trends that used to be popular will become popular again in the future. Do you agree? Give some examples of trends that have returned.

2 Do you think achieving success in the fashion industry requires more talent or hard work? What skills would you need to succeed?

3 Have you heard of the phrase *being a slave to fashion*? What do you think it means?

Disappearing Animals

Getting Ready

Discuss the following questions with a partner.

1 Match these names with the animals in the picture.

> **a** great auk   **b** thylacine (Tasmanian tiger)   **c** quagga
> **d** dodo   **e** giant ground sloth   **f** passenger pigeon

2 Have you heard of any of these animals before? What do you know about them?

3 What do you think these animals have in common?

CHAPTER 1 Endangered Species

Before You Read
Valuing Wildlife

A **What are some reasons for protecting wildlife? Rank the following from 1–5 (1 = most important).**

_____ They make the world a more beautiful place.
_____ They are valuable in the research and creation of medicines.
_____ They have rights, and humans must respect them.
_____ They are important to science and our understanding of the Earth.
_____ They are essential to keeping nature and the ecosystem in balance.

B **Discuss your answers with a partner.**

Reading Skill
Identifying Meaning from Context

To guess the meaning of an important but unfamiliar word in a passage, try the following strategy: First, look at the different parts of the word to see whether there are any clues to its meaning. Second, notice the word's part of speech. Third, look at the words and sentences around the new word for synonyms, antonyms, or a definition.

A **Read the following extract from the article on the pages 41–42. Then choose the best definition for the word in blue.**

No animal species can survive indefinitely on Earth. Centuries ago, species went extinct from natural causes, for example, they were unable to adapt to bad weather and other hard conditions. However, animals are now dying out faster than ever because of human activity.

The word indefinitely means _____ .
a with great difficulty
b without an end or limit
c with an aim or purpose

B **Now scan the article for the words in blue. Read the sentence containing the word and some of the surrounding sentences. Then choose the best definition.**

1 In line 30, the word culprits means _____ .
  a competitors **b** victims **c** causes
2 In line 53, the word intentionally means _____ .
  a purposely **b** cruelly **c** innocently
3 In line 59, the word overwhelm means to _____ .
  a destroy **b** fight with **c** support

C **Read the entire passage carefully. Then answer the questions on page 43.**

Endangered Species

No animal species[1] can survive **indefinitely** on Earth. Centuries ago, species went extinct from natural causes, for example, they were unable to adapt to bad weather and other difficult conditions. However, animals are now dying out faster than ever because of human activity. It is estimated that, until the 18th century,
5 one species disappeared from the Earth every four years. By the 19th century, this had increased to one species per year. By 1975, it was 1,000 species per year, and today animals are disappearing at the alarming rate of more than 40,000 species per year.

The International Union for Conservation of Nature (IUCN) has created a number
10 of categories that describe the danger level of animal species.

- Species that are completely gone are called *extinct*, for example, dinosaurs and the dodo.

- Species that only live in zoos or on farms, etc., fall into the category *extinct in the wild*. One example is the Wyoming toad.

15 - A species is labeled **critically** *endangered* when its numbers are dangerously low. This means it is in **imminent** danger of dying out completely and needs protection in order to survive. The Siberian tiger and the snow leopard are two examples.

20 - Species that have a high, but not immediate, risk of dying out are simply labeled *endangered*. The giant panda is a famous example.

Wyoming toad

- A vulnerable species is in less trouble than an endangered one, but its numbers are still **markedly** declining. The cheetah
25 and the African elephant are *vulnerable* species.

- Animal species that are considered *of least concern* aren't particularly endangered and have high numbers of individuals.

[1] A **species** is a group of animals or plants that are very similar and can reproduce together.

There are many factors that can cause an animal or plant species to become endangered, and one big one is the destruction of their habitats. Deforestation and soil, air, and water pollution are usually the main **culprits**. For example, the population of critically endangered Sumatran orangutans is now less than 10,000 on their home island of Sumatra, Indonesia, due to deforestation and farming.

A policeman in India showing elephant tusks taken from poachers.

Another cause of endangerment is from humans **exploiting** wild animals. Uncontrolled hunting of whales in the last century, for example, resulted in many whale species becoming critically endangered. The high demand for animal parts stems from their use in certain foods or medicines or their value as decorative objects. For example, the ivory tusks of elephants are used to make jewelry, and the price is high enough that people risk being arrested and jailed to go after these animals.

Introducing a non-native species to an environment can also cause species endangerment. A native species is one that develops naturally in a particular area and has done so for a long time. A non-native species might be introduced into a new environment by humans, either **intentionally** or by accident. The brown tree snake, unknowingly brought by cargo ships[2] stopping at Guam, has managed to kill off ten

of the eleven species of birds native to the island's forests. In Florida, large pet snakes such as the anaconda and the python have been released into the large Everglades swamp. The snakes have thrived in their new environment, and now compete with and may soon **overwhelm** the swamp's alligators.

Organizations such as the World Wildlife Fund and the IUCN try to raise awareness of threatened animals and plants. These organizations collaborate with government agencies to save threatened or endangered species and to make new laws that will protect them. But to really protect plant and animal species now and in the future, the public needs to be educated on the value of keeping these species alive.

[2] A **cargo ship** is any sort of ship or vessel that carries goods and materials from one place to another.

A Choose the correct answer for the following questions.

1 According to the passage, what happened between the 18th century and now?
   a The amount of human activity increased.
   b Animals were less able to adapt to the weather.
   c More animals started dying from natural causes.

2 Why have many whale species become endangered?
   a Their habitat is being destroyed.
   b They have been hunted in great numbers.
   c A non-native species has been introduced to their environment.

3 Which is NOT mentioned as a cause of species endangerment?
   a spread of diseases
   b habitat destruction
   c unrestricted hunting

4 Which animal is native to the Everglades swamp?
   a anacondas   b pythons   c alligators

5 What is the main idea of the final paragraph?
   a Governments and organizations must work together to be effective.
   b The most important thing is to raise awareness and educate people.
   c Laws are needed to protect these endangered species.

B Read the following sentences about various animals. Write whether the animal is *extinct, extinct in the wild, critically endangered, endangered, vulnerable,* or *of less concern*. Then discuss your answers with a partner.

1 There were about 100,000 koalas in 2008, but their numbers have noticeably declined due to environmental changes.

   _____

2 Lonesome George, the last Pinta Island tortoise, died in 2012.

   _____

3 As of October 2012, only 190 Hawaiian Crows remain, in two breeding facilities run by the San Diego Zoo.

   _____

4 The minke whale lives in almost all of the world's oceans and is the most commonly sighted species in whale-watching expeditions.

   _____

5 There are so few Visayan warty pigs in the wild that conservationists are now trying to breed them in zoos.

   _____

C Discuss the following questions with a partner.

Critical Thinking

1 Why do you think the IUCN creates categories for animals?
2 Do you think most people are concerned about endangered species? Why, or why not?

Vocabulary Comprehension

Odd Word Out

A (Circle) the word or phrase that does not belong in each group. The words in blue are from the passage.

1	inadequate	overwhelming	lacking	scarce
2	indefinite	unlimited	not defined	distinct
3	victim	culprit	suspect	criminal
4	critical	momentary	vital	key
5	strikingly	markedly	noticeably	secretly
6	imminent	approaching	departing	oncoming
7	mistakenly	intentionally	accidentally	unknowingly
8	wipe out	destroy	exploit	finish off

B Complete the following sentences using the words in blue from **A**. You might have to change the form of the word.

1 You will notice Lars by his height; he is _____ taller than his classmates.

2 The stress was so _____ that he broke down and cried.

3 Due to the _____ hurricane, school has been cancelled tomorrow for two days.

4 One cause of global warming is production of greenhouse gases; the other big _____ is smoke from vehicles.

5 He _____ left the dinner early so he would not have to pay the bill.

6 Some people feel we are at a(n) _____ point in history when it comes to global warming. We need to take action before it's too late.

7 The tour has been delayed _____ because the drummer left the band.

8 He may be willing to pay for your meals, but you shouldn't _____ the situation and ask him out for dinner all the time!

A Use *en-* or *em-* to complete the words in the sentences below. Discuss your answers with a partner.

1 James was convinced that his new haircut _____hanced his good looks.
2 Education _____powers people to make the right choices.
3 The couple stopped arguing and _____braced each other.
4 The scientist used a microscope to _____large the image of the cells.
5 Rupert had the date of his wedding _____graved on the inside of his wedding ring.

B Complete the following sentences using the correct form of the *en-* words in the box. You may use a dictionary to help you.

enclose   embed   enable   embody   enforce

1 The CEO of a company needs to _____ all the values that the company stands for.
2 If the teacher doesn't _____ classroom rules from day one, he or she will never have control.
3 There are bullets _____ in the wall as evidence of the war.
4 When you mail the warranty card to the electronics company, be sure to _____ a copy of your receipt.
5 This new password feature will _____ users to protect sensitive information.

Vocabulary Skill
The Prefixes *en-* and *em-*

In this chapter you read the word *endangered*, which begins with the prefix *en-*, meaning *(to put) into* or *to cover*. When *en-* comes before *b* or *p*, it changes to *em-*.

Motivational Tip: Are you applying yourself? Are you giving your best effort? When we are honest with ourselves, we often recognize that we could be doing more to achieve our best. On a scale of 1–10 (1 = low effort, 10 = high effort) where would you rate yourself in terms of applying your effort during this unit? If your effort falls between 7–10, congratulations, you are doing well. If your effort falls below 7, what could you do to apply yourself more?

CHAPTER 2 Bring Back the Woolly Mammoth?

Before You Read
Animal Conservation

A **Answer the following questions.**

1 What is happening in the image above?
2 What do you know about animal conservation? What are some methods of animal conservation?
3 Does your country have any endangered species? What is the government doing to save them?

B **Discuss your answers with a partner.**

Reading Skill
Identifying Main Ideas within Paragraphs

Many paragraphs are constructed around a main idea. This idea is usually presented in a sentence within the paragraph. Quickly finding the main idea will increase your speed of reading and comprehension.

A **Skim the passage on the pages 47–48 quickly, then read the following sentences. Circle the main idea for each paragraph.**

Paragraph 2
a The species mentioned in the paragraph lived in different times.
b There are a number of extinct species that scientists want to revive.

Paragraph 3
a There are two possible ways to go about reviving extinct species.
b Scientists can use sex cells to revive extinct animals.

Paragraph 4
a Cloning has been done but only to a very small extent.
b Quite a few problems still prevent species from being revived.

Paragraph 5
a It may be ethically wrong to bring back extinct species.
b A single individual of a revived species would have no parents.

B **Discuss your answers with a partner. Then skim the passage to check if your answers are correct.**

C **Read the entire passage carefully. Then answer the questions on page 49.**

Bring Back the Woolly Mammoth?

1 Scientists estimate that throughout the course of Earth's history, more than a billion different species of animals and insects have existed. Today, there are only about 30–50
5 million species left, according to the World Animal Foundation. That means that for every species living on Earth today, 20 more are already extinct. Scientists study extinct species to get a better understanding of
10 the past. In addition to studying what these species might have been like when they were alive, some scientists are interested in the possibility of seeing some of them walk the Earth again.

2

the New Zealand moa

There are a number of serious proposals to try to **revive** extinct species. Some animals on this 15 list include: the woolly mammoth (an elephant-like creature that wandered the plains of Siberia), the moa (a giant flightless bird from New Zealand), the thylacine 20 (also known as the Tasmanian tiger because of the dark stripes down its back), and the bucardo (a mountain goat from Spain). These animals had very little in common and in most cases lived **eras** apart. The woolly mammoth, for example, died many thousands of
25 years ago while the bucardo became extinct only around the year 2000. But all these species lived at the same time as humans, and humans have been largely responsible for their destruction. So it seems somehow **fitting** that we are now thinking of reviving them.

3 Scientists have proposed reviving an extinct species using two possible methods. In
30 the first method, sex cells (sperm or eggs) are obtained from the extinct animal and are used to fertilize sex cells of a closely related living relative in a laboratory. For example,

sperm from a woolly mammoth could be used to fertilize an egg from a modern-day elephant. The fertilized egg would then be placed in the live female elephant where it would live and grow until it is ready to be born. The second method involves a type of

35 cloning. In cloning, the DNA of one individual replaces the DNA of another. In the woolly mammoth example, scientists could **inject** DNA from a mammoth into an egg cell from an elephant. The cloned egg cell would then be placed into a living elephant and allowed to develop in the same way as a fertilized egg.

4   But some scientists believe species
40 revival will never happen because both methods are problematic. One of the major challenges is how to obtain enough high-quality DNA from an extinct species to **conduct** an experiment. While it
45 is theoretically possible under ideal conditions to preserve genetic material for thousands of years, these conditions rarely occur in real life. For example,

Dolly the sheep was the first animal to ever be cloned.

researchers have obtained a number of samples of mammoth DNA, but none
50 have been usable. And the cloning process presents its own problems. Scientists have been able to clone only a few species of animals, and most cloned creatures are **frail** and don't live very long.

5   And there is a final, ethical consideration. Even if we learn how to reproduce an example of an extinct species, that individual could never have a normal life. Its
55 natural environment is most likely gone and it would have no parents to show it how to behave as a member of its species. So the animal would remain a curiosity and probably live out its life in a zoo. People question whether it would be ethical to revive one of nature's creatures for such a purpose.

6   Only time will tell if scientists manage to carry out their ambitious plans. Even if
60 they manage to overcome the scientific problems, they may face **opposition** from governments or society. Some even feel it might be more **worthwhile** for us to focus our efforts on conservation and take care of existing species, so they don't also go the way of the woolly mammoth.

A **Choose the correct answers for the following questions.**

1 Which statement is true regarding the number of species on Earth?
   a At one point, there used to be over a billion species living on Earth.
   b There are more extinct species than there are living species.
   c About 20 species of animals are going extinct every day.

2 What does the sentence *So it seems somehow fitting that we are now thinking of reviving them* (lines 27–28) mean?
   a These species deserve to be revived because they died of unnatural causes.
   b Only humans have the intelligence and ability to revive these extinct species.
   c Since humans contributed to their extinction, humans should also be responsible for their revival.

3 Both methods require _____.
   a the DNA of the extinct species
   b the sperm of the extinct species
   c a living species that is closely related to the extinct species

4 Which is NOT true about revived animals?
   a They will look different from the original members of their species.
   b They will probably be kept in zoos and conservation centers.
   c They will probably behave differently from how they originally did.

5 What is the overall message of the article?
   a People are sure to say no to species revival due to ethical issues.
   b There are many issues to consider when it comes to species revival.
   c It is highly unlikely that scientists will succeed in reviving extinct animals.

B **Read the following sentences. Check (✓) whether they are true (T) or false (F).**

	T	F
1 Studying extinct species can help us understand the past.		
2 The moa is known for the dark stripes down its back.		
3 The bucardo died out before the woolly mammoth did.		
4 Both methods require the extinct species to develop from an egg.		
5 Scientists have successfully managed to preserve mammoth DNA.		
6 People may not want to see extinct species revived.		

Critical Thinking

C Discuss the following questions with a partner.

1 The passage mentions several reasons against reviving extinct animals. What are some reasons to support reviving them?

2 If reviving extinct animals were possible, which one would you bring back? Why?

Vocabulary Comprehension
Words in Context

A Choose the best answer. The words in blue are from the passage.

1 What can you conduct?
   a an experiment   b a car

2 To inject is to _____.
   a take something out   b put something in

3 When we say "the end of an era," we mean the end of a _____.
   a ten-year period   b certain period of time

4 A worthwhile task is one that _____.
   a is beneficial   b takes a lot of time

5 The opposition is likely to say _____ to our proposal.
   a yes   b no

6 An outfit that is fitting for the occasion _____.
   a matches the dress code   b looks good on the person

7 If someone is in frail health, he or she _____.
   a exercises regularly   b becomes sick easily

8 I revived my enthusiasm for playing piano because I _____.
   a used to love playing as a child b would like to learn

B Complete the following sentences using the words in blue from A. You might have to change the form of the word.

1 He fainted and we had to _____ him by splashing water on his face.

2 There was a lot of _____ to the government's plan to build a highway next to a residential area.

3 Organizing my mom's birthday party was hard work but it was all _____ when I saw how happy she was.

4 In the wild, animals that are _____ are the most vulnerable to attack.

5 The teacher is going to _____ a class survey to find our level of awareness about endangered species.

6 The nurse used a needle to _____ medicine into the patient's arm.

7 Since Peter was the one who introduced the couple, it was _____ that he was the best man for the wedding.

8 The development of antibiotics marked a new _____ in modern medicine.

A Complete the following sentences using the words in the box. You might have to change the form of the word.

commercialize	hospitalize	idolize	legalize	stabilize	digitize	authorize

1 Thousands of teen girls _____ that rock star.
2 Many elderly people were _____ for heatstroke during the long, hot summer.
3 Alcohol used to be banned in the United States. It was _____ in 1933.
4 You must sign this form in order to _____ the payment.
5 Radio stations are so _____ nowadays; there are more advertisements than music!
6 The banks are waiting for the economy to _____ before they make any big decisions.
7 I would like to _____ my music collection so I can put it on my portable music player.

B Add the suffix *-ize* to the words in the box, then use them to complete the following sentences. You might have to change the form of the word. You may use a dictionary to help you.

modern	sterile	final	energy	colony	summary

1 Drinking a cup of coffee in the morning always _____ me.
2 I can't show you the party plans until I _____ them.
3 You can use alcohol or iodine to _____ a wound.
4 The government is taking steps to _____ the country's communications networks so people can have faster Internet access.
5 Many Asian countries were _____ by European countries in the 19th century.
6 One good reading skill is to be able to _____ the passage accurately after reading.

Motivational Tip: Using this vocabulary skill in your reading. This vocabulary skill of being able to recognize words with the suffix *-ize* will help you in your reading beyond this book. How can you utilize this in your reading outside of class? If you don't practice this skill, you will eventually forget it. So try out your new skill outside of the classroom and your vocabulary will continue to increase!

Real Life Skill

Dictionary Usage:
Choosing the Right Word

In English, there are many words or phrases that are similar in meaning but are not exactly the same. In a good English-English dictionary, there will often be usage notes that compare the word or phrase with another, or explain how the word or phrase is used. Using these notes can help you choose the correct word or phrase.

A Read the dictionary entries below. Explain to a partner how the words *dead*, *extinct*, *exotic* and *foreign* are similar and different.

> **dead** *adj.*   no longer living, lifeless: *I think this plant is dead.*
> **ex•tinct** *adj.*   something that is no longer in existence, specifically used for animals, plants, or ideas: *Dinosaurs became extinct about 60 million years ago.*

> **ex•ot•ic** *adj.*   different, strange, foreign, usually in an interesting or exciting way: *Carmen prepared an exotic dish from southern Spain.*
> **for•eign** *adj.*   located outside one's native country or area; non-native, different: *Hiroko speaks Japanese and two foreign languages.*

B Complete the following sentences with one of the words from **A**.

1 I've traveled all over my own country and, in addition, have visited five _____ countries.

2 There were once many dodos on the island of Mauritius. Since the late 1800s, though, the bird has been _____.

3 I thought that Cary Grant, the actor, was still alive, but someone told me that he's been _____ for more than ten years.

4 Many people think the white tiger is a(n) _____ and beautiful animal.

C Think of a synonym for a new word or phrase you learned in this unit. Can the word or phrase and its synonym be used in exactly the same way? You may use a dictionary to help you.

What do you think?

1 Are there any endangered species in your country? What is the government doing to protect them? What can you do as an individual to help save endangered animals?

2 Why are some animals more successful than others in terms of survival? Can you give any examples?

3 Some people believe animals that are unable to adapt to the changing environment should be allowed to go extinct. What do you think?

Fluency Strategy: DRTA

When you begin reading you should ask yourself, "Why am I reading this? What do I hope to learn?" Reading comprehension improves when you read with a purpose. **D**irected **R**eading **T**hinking **A**ctivity (DRTA) is a strategy that will help you to read critically and purposefully. Each stage of the DRTA procedure has four steps: Predicting, Reading, Proving, and Reasoning.

Predicting

Read the title and first sentence of the passage on page 55 below, and look at the photo. Make predictions (or hypotheses) about what you will read about in the passage. For example, what do you think "ecotourism" involves? What kind of effects might it have?

Ecotourism

Ecotourism is a combination of *ecology* (the study of systems of living things) and *tourism*.

Reading

Now read the first two paragraphs of the passage. As you read, consider whether your predictions were accurate.

The word *ecotourism* is a combination of *ecology* (the study of systems of living things) and *tourism*. The International Ecotourism Society defines ecotourism as "responsible travel to natural areas that conserves the environment and improves the well-being of the local people." This means that walking through a rain forest isn't really ecotourism unless it benefits the area, perhaps by providing jobs to the local residents or by conserving the wildlife. Countries are slowly recognizing that it is possible to make money while preserving their natural resources.

Costa Rica has been leading the ecotourism movement for some time, and was voted the most popular ecotourism destination by TripAdvisor.com in April 2012. It developed the Certification for Sustainable Tourism (CST) program in 1999, which was then used by the United Nations World Tourism Organization as the model for the rest of Latin America. Thanks to its conservation efforts, over 25 percent of Costa Rica's land is covered in lush national parks. Its tourism industry generates over a billion dollars annually and provides jobs to thousands of people.

Proving

When you have finished reading the first two paragraphs, discuss what you learned with a partner. Read aloud the parts of the passage that relate to your predictions. Were your predictions accurate? Do you need to revise them?

_____

_____

Reasoning

Now, based on what you have learned so far, make new predictions. What do you think you'll read about in the next two paragraphs? Why do you think so?

_____

_____

Continue using the steps *Reading*, *Proving*, and *Reasoning* until you have finished the entire passage. Then, with a partner, summarize the main points you have learned about ecotourism.

_____

_____

_____

_____

Ecotourism

ecotourists cruising around Bear Island, Norway

1 The word *ecotourism* is a combination of *ecology* (the study of systems of living things) and *tourism*. The International Ecotourism Society defines ecotourism as "responsible travel to
5 natural areas that conserves the environment and improves the well-being of the local people." This means that walking through a rain forest isn't really ecotourism unless it benefits the area, perhaps by providing jobs to the local residents
10 or by conserving the wildlife. Countries are slowly recognizing that it is possible to make money while preserving their natural resources.

ecotourists in Monteverde Cloud Forest Preserve, Costa Rica

2

Nature photographers Michael and Patricia Fogden pose with their photos of the extinct golden toad in Costa Rica.

3

Costa Rica has been leading the ecotourism movement for some time, and was voted the most popular ecotourism destination by TripAdvisor.com in April 2012. 15 It developed the Certification for Sustainable Tourism (CST) program in 1999, which was then used by the United Nations World Tourism Organization as the model for the rest of Latin America. Thanks to its conservation efforts, over 25 percent of Costa Rica's land is covered 20 in lush national parks. Its tourism industry generates over a billion dollars annually and provides jobs to thousands of people.

Unfortunately, people in the industry sometimes exploit the "ecotourism" label in their drive for profit. 25 This brand of ecotourism isn't always conducted in the most responsible way, and may damage the very environment it seeks to protect. One concern is that the overwhelming number of visitors to these natural

places (especially in the high season) has a negative effect on the ecosystem. Ecotourists tend to seek out places with the rarest animals and plants; even if they take care not to disturb the environment, their presence could put pressure on the most frail of living things. Another problem is the interaction between animals and humans. At one national park in Costa Rica, wild monkeys feed on garbage left by the visitors and even aggressively steal food from tourists.

4 Controlling abuses isn't easy, either. In developing countries where salaries aren't high, corruption can lead officials to tolerate ecological damage. For example, a large resort facility, normally not allowed near a sanctuary, might be allowed if the company bribes (gives money to) certain people in the government. Limited resources are another issue—areas of forests and beaches that would require an army to protect are often watched by just a few employees.

5 While tourists can have a negative impact on ecosystems, the same areas might have been totally destroyed by industries such as farming, logging, or mining if the ecotourism industry did not exist. Tour guides can also be educators who train people to love and care for the environment. By visiting these beautiful rain forests and seeing rare animals, visitors get a sense of their value and will hopefully take these lessons back with them to their home countries.

observing gentoo penguins in Antarctica

6 It is easy to be critical of the ecotourism industry, but it is important to be positive as well. Ecotourism can never be "pure"—we can't expect zero negative effects on the ecosystem. It is also unrealistic to think that humans won't go anywhere accessible to them. If protection efforts are maintained and intensified, those remaining places of undisturbed nature may be stressed, but at least they won't be destroyed.

Check how well you understood the passage by answering the following questions.

1 Which statement best summarizes the author's point of view?
   a Ecotourism is a damaging trend that must be stopped.
   b Ecotourism is the best way for countries to earn tourist dollars.
   c Ecotourism generally benefits ecosystems, even if it causes some damage.
   d Ecotourism will most likely become less popular in the future.

2 Which change has NOT occurred in Costa Rica since the introduction of ecotourism?
   a Thousands of ecotourism-related jobs have been created.
   b New national parks have been created.
   c Monkeys have started feeding on garbage.
   d The number of corruption cases has decreased.

3 What is the main idea of paragraph 3?
   a Places with the rarest animals and plants are the most popular with ecotourists.
   b More countries are getting into ecotourism because it is big business.
   c Ecotourism can cause damage to the environment if conducted in an irresponsible way.
   d Ecotourists should not be allowed to interact with wildlife at all.

4 According to paragraph 4, why is it difficult to control abuses of ecotourism?
   a Too many sanctuaries are being created.
   b There aren't enough resources and officials may overlook abuses if bribed.
   c Not many people are interested in jobs controlling ecotourism abuses.
   d Companies have a lot of power and money to build resorts.

5 *In this way, the children of future generations can learn respect for nature*. This sentence is best inserted at the end of _____.
   a Paragraph 3
   b Paragraph 4
   c Paragraph 5
   d Paragraph 6

6 The word *corruption* in line 40 is closest in meaning to _____.
   a illegal activity
   b lack of resources
   c government control
   d management

7 *It is easy to be critical of the ecotourism industry* (lines 53–54). What does the writer mean by this?
   a Wildlife is very easy to protect.
   b Businesses will always want to exploit nature.
   c People's expectations for ecotourism are too high.
   d Ecotourism can't create enough jobs for local people.

SELF CHECK

Answer the following questions.

1 Have you ever used the DRTA method before?

☐ Yes ☐ No ☐ *I'm not sure.*

2 Will you practice DRTA in your reading outside of English class?

☐ Yes ☐ No ☐ *I'm not sure.*

3 Do you think DRTA is helpful? Why or why not?

_____

_____

4 Which of the six reading passages in units 1–3 did you enjoy most? Why?

_____

_____

5 Which of the six reading passages in units 1–3 was easiest? Which was the most difficult? Why?

_____

_____

6 What have you read in English outside of class recently?

_____

_____

7 Do you usually think about your purpose for reading before you read something? Why, or why not?

_____

_____

8 How will you try to improve your reading fluency from now on?

_____

_____

Review Reading 1: The Globalization of Fashion

Fluency Practice

Time yourself as you read through the passage. Write down your time, then answer the questions on page 61. After answering the questions, correct your responses and write down your score. Record your performance on the Reading Rate Chart on page 240.

THE GLOBALIZATION OF FASHION

1 Walk down any shopping street in a big city and you'll see big names such as Zara, H&M, Gap, or Nike. A dress bought from one of these stores will be exactly
5 the same as in another store halfway around the world. Indeed, fashion is one of the most globalized industries, with giant retailers who can create new designs, send them to be manufactured,
10 and then distributed to stores around the world—all with the click of a mouse or a simple phone call.

2 For consumers in developed countries, globalization means an abundance of choice. This is the era of "fast fashion," where designs can go from the design board to factories to stores in two weeks. It is also "fast" in the sense that it takes
15 less time for trends to come and go. Historically, the price of clothes has never been lower and this, combined with the ever-changing stock, encourages people to follow the latest fashions and change their wardrobes more frequently.

3 However, the speed and low price of fashion can come at a cost. For consumers, it may result in poor quality fabrics and badly-made clothes that fall apart after
20 being worn several times. Then there is a much heavier cost—one that involves the people who actually make the clothes. Many big multinational companies do not manufacture their own goods, but sign contracts with manufacturers to produce them. These manufacturers then source and engage factories in developing countries for tasks like sewing and cutting. Because poverty is high, these factories
25 can exploit the workers and pay them wages that are as low as 23 cents an hour.

4 A government investigation into factories manufacturing Zara clothes revealed that it cost Inditex (the company that owns Zara) about $1.14 to manufacture a pair of jeans selling at $126. This $1.14 doesn't go straight to the worker who makes

the clothes, but is divided among the parties involved in the entire production process. Although the minimum wage in Brazil is $344, these factory workers only earned between $156 and $290 a month. Renato Bignami, who led the investigation, said: "They work 16 or even 18 hours a day. It is extremely exhausting work, from Monday to Saturday, sometimes even Sunday depending on demand."

workers in a garment factory

5 But supporters of this globalized labor process argue that retail companies are not the main culprits since, without them, many people in developing countries would be without a job. They also feel that it's impossible for companies to monitor all the factories that work for them, and that responsibility to enforce labor laws should lie with the government. Consumers are also responsible, even if unintentionally. By choosing to buy cheaper clothes, they force brands to lower their prices to compete against each other, which in turn forces manufacturers to drive wages down.

6 The hope is that consumers are able to use their spending power to convince companies to take a more ethical route, for example, by giving contracts to manufacturers with good track records in how they treat their employees. In the late 1990s, sports brand Nike came under pressure when campaigners exposed what went on in the factories making its products. This included child labor, unsafe working conditions including exposure to dangerous chemicals, low pay, and very long working hours. All the negative publicity, including a long-running campaign to boycott the brand, finally forced Nike to take action, for example, by conducting regular factory inspections.

protesting against Nike

7 Globalization is not necessarily a bad thing, but the many layers and processes involved in producing goods certainly encourages exploitation and helps companies avoid responsibility for any wrongdoing. In the end, it's important that consumers are aware of what goes into producing their clothes and choose responsible and ethical companies when it comes to spending their money.

627 words   **Time taken** _____

Reading Comprehension

1 What is the overall message of this article?
  a We should try to shop less.
  b We should question where our clothes come from.
  c We should pay more for our clothes.
  d We should not participate in the "fast fashion" trend.

2 Which is NOT an example of "fast fashion"?
  a A dress modeled on the catwalk is available in stores after a week.
  b A consumer throws out last year's clothes and buys the latest fashions.
  c A company is quick to react when people complain about its clothes.
  d A fashion trend dies out quickly and is followed by a new one.

3 When it comes to producing clothes, most big companies _____ .
  a own and manage their own factories
  b prefer to employ people in developed countries
  c get manufacturers to locate factories on their behalf
  d prefer to do the sewing and cutting themselves

4 According to paragraph 4, how much does a worker earn for each pair of jeans?
  a less than $1.14
  b $1.14
  c $126
  d $156

5 *Retail companies are not the main culprits* (lines 38–39). Which reason supports this argument?
  a They don't have control over which manufacturers they use.
  b They actually pay employees very well.
  c They carefully monitor all their factories.
  d They are responding to customer demands for cheap clothes.

6 According to the passage, what is the best way consumers can protest against unethical companies?
  a They should buy more expensive clothes.
  b They should write to the companies and complain.
  c They should demand the government launch more investigations.
  d They should not buy clothes from such companies.

7 *Regardless of whose fault it is, the people who suffer most are the factory workers*. This sentence is best inserted at the end of _____ .
  a Paragraph 3
  b Paragraph 4
  c Paragraph 5
  d Paragraph 6

Fluency Practice

Time yourself as you read through the passage. Write down your time, then answer the questions on page 64. After answering the questions, correct your responses and write down your score. Record your performance on the Reading Rate Chart on page 240.

ANIMAL SUCCESS STORIES

In 1973, the United States government passed into law the Endangered Species Act (ESA). Its three major goals were: 1. to protect plants and animals from extinction by listing them as endangered; 2. to preserve the habitat of these species; 3. to help populations of listed species recover. Because of these
5 conservation efforts, many animals have been brought back from near extinction. Here are three such success stories.

Bald eagle

It is fitting that we begin with the story of the bald eagle, the national symbol of the United States. There was an
10 abundance of bald eagles in North America before the arrival of Europeans, numbering an estimated half a million birds. By 1963, however, the population had dropped to fewer than 1,000. Hunting was certainly a major factor in this decline, as was the destruction of habitat. But the
15 biggest factor was DDT—a chemical widely used in insect sprays. It had a damaging effect on the eagles' eggs, making their shells so thin so that they broke easily and exposed the frail baby birds inside which die soon after.

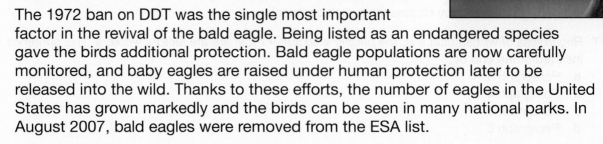

The 1972 ban on DDT was the single most important
20 factor in the revival of the bald eagle. Being listed as an endangered species gave the birds additional protection. Bald eagle populations are now carefully monitored, and baby eagles are raised under human protection later to be released into the wild. Thanks to these efforts, the number of eagles in the United States has grown markedly and the birds can be seen in many national parks. In
25 August 2007, bald eagles were removed from the ESA list.

Grizzly bear

Another classic symbol of North American wildlife is the grizzly bear. Before the Europeans arrived, more than 50,000 grizzlies wandered the American West. Today, due to hunting and habitat destruction, that number is closer to 1,000.

Furthermore, because grizzly bears have babies at a very slow rate, it takes many years for the population to grow.   30

Most of the grizzly bears in the United States, excluding Alaska, live in Yellowstone and Glacier National Parks.   35
As grizzlies are still protected by the ESA, hunting them is illegal. As bear populations grow, it becomes very important to prevent encounters between humans and bears: 20 to 40 bears are killed each year to protect the safety of humans. People living in grizzly bear habitats are encouraged not to leave garbage lying around in case bears are attracted to the smell, and parks put up signs warning people not to stray off the path. Visitors are also warned not to alarm any bears they encounter.   40 ... 45

Gray wolf

Finally, the gray or timber wolf's story is one of the most compelling tales of American wildlife. Traditionally shunned because people fear them and consider them pests for killing livestock, gray wolves have been shot, trapped, and poisoned, even in nature reserves. By the time the gray wolf was declared a protected species in 1973, only a   50 ... 55
few hundred remained in small pockets of the country. Today, the gray wolf population has been revived in some of its former habitats, like Yellowstone National Park, due to strong conservation efforts. They have also started returning to places like Washington and Idaho. The gray wolf is now listed as a species of *least concern* by IUCN.   60

In 2006, the United States government declared May 11 to be Endangered Species Day—a day devoted to raising awareness of endangered species. With such positive steps toward educating people on the importance of conservation, there's reason to be optimistic about the future of endangered animals in the U.S.   65

596 words   **Time taken _____**

Reading Comprehension

1 What was the author's main purpose in writing this article?
   a to celebrate government successes in helping endangered animals
   b to instruct people in the United States about how to save animals
   c to point out the causes of animal endangerment
   d to encourage people to send money to help animals

2 What is NOT mentioned as a goal of the Endangered Species Act?
   a listing animals and plants as endangered
   b preserving plant and animal habitats
   c helping endangered species populations to grow
   d developing national parks

3 What was the most destructive factor for bald eagle populations?
   a hunting
   b loss of habitat
   c the use of DDT
   d the slow birth rate

4 Which is NOT mentioned as a way to prevent unnecessary grizzly bear deaths?
   a better garbage management
   b keeping people in safe and bear-free areas
   c restricting people from entering national parks
   d advising people on what to do if they see a grizzly

5 Why were so many gray wolves killed before 1973?
   a They had a bad reputation.
   b People hunted them for their fur.
   c Their habitats were destroyed.
   d There were too many in the nature reserves.

6 Which is NOT true about the three animals highlighted in the article?
   a They were all affected by the new ESA in 1973.
   b They can all be found in various national parks.
   c They are all well-known animals in North America.
   d They are all no longer protected by the ESA.

7 Which statement is the author most likely to agree with?
   a The U.S. government is not doing enough for animal conservation.
   b The future for endangered animals is looking uncertain in the U.S.
   c Endangered Species Day is more important than the Endangered Species Act.
   d Raising awareness of animal conservation is a very important step.

Getting Ready

Discuss the following questions with a partner.

1 What has happened to the man in the above picture?
2 Is there a lottery system in your country? How much money can you win?
3 Finish this sentence: *If I won a million dollars, I would . . .*

CHAPTER 1 What Does a Million
Dollars Buy?

Before You Read
Money Knowledge

A The following graph charts the price of the same basket of goods in the U.S. over a period of a few decades starting from 1950. How has time affected the price of goods? What does this tell you about inflation?

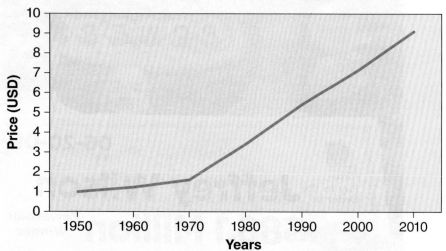

B Discuss your ideas in **A** with a partner. How much do you think a million dollars is worth today compared to 20 years ago? How about 50 years ago?

Reading Skill
Identifying Cause and Effect

Words and phrases such as *because, due to (the fact that), as a result, so,* and *in order to* are used to show a cause-and-effect relationship; they signal that one thing (cause) makes another thing (effect) happen. Recognizing cause and effect can help you better understand and organize the information in a passage.

A Skim the passage on the pages 67–68. Then write the cause (reason) or effect (result) for each problem below. Discuss your answers with a partner.

	Cause	Effect
1	The population is more dense, but there are fewer homes available.	Housing has become very expensive.
2		People started moving to the suburbs.
3	People want to be closer to their workplace.	
4		We need more money to buy things.
5	Many older people are living longer.	

B <u>Underline</u> the words and phrases in the passage that helped you understand the cause-and-effect relationships in **A**.

C Now read the entire passage carefully. Then answer the questions on page 69.

What Does a Million Dollars Buy?

1 When asked the question "What would you do with a million dollars?" most people tend to give similar answers: "Quit my job," "Buy my dream house," or "Go traveling." People often think that having a million dollars would make all their dreams come true. **In reality**, a million dollars may not really be that much money.

5 Twenty years ago, it might have been possible to **fulfill** these dreams. However, things are not so easy today.

2 In most industrialized[1] countries, prices for everything from food to transport to university fees have steadily increased over the years. Housing prices in particular have risen greatly. The main reason is that the population has increased—becoming

10 very **dense** in certain areas—but there are fewer homes available for sale or rent. For example, in the U.S., the average price of a new home in 1990 was $149,800. The average price in 2010 was $272,900. With increases like that, you can see why owning **property** is considered a good long-term **investment**.

The world's most expensive home is in South Mumbai. It is said to be worth $1 billion and belongs to Indian businessman Mukesh Ambani.

3 15 Housing in city centers also costs more than ever before. People used to move from the city center to the outer city neighborhoods or suburbs to escape overcrowding and noise. Today, many are moving back because they want

20 to be closer to their workplace. Since space is limited in these areas, supply has not caught up with rising demand, and prices have gone up a result. For example, it is nearly impossible to find a place in London's expensive Mayfair district, or

25 Manhattan in New York City, for a million dollars. Even countries that traditionally have a lower cost of living, like India or Brazil, have seen property prices rise dramatically. A 2,000 square foot

[1] An **industrialized** country is one that is highly developed and has high standards of living.

(186 square meter) apartment in Mumbai's southern neighborhoods can cost more
30 than $3 million—the same as a two-bedroom flat in central London.

4 **Inflation** is another important reason for the rise in the cost of living. Over the
last 150 years, as prices have gone up, the value of money has gone down, so we
now need more money to buy things. In 1913, for example, $50,000 had about as
much buying power as $1 million does today. Of course, people
now earn more money than they did 150 years ago, but they also 35
spend more on **necessities** such as food,
medicine, and housing. Due to this increased
cost of living and a tendency for younger
generations to spend more, people are actually
saving less than ever before. 40

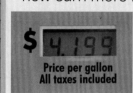

Price per gallon
All taxes included

The price of oil has risen dramatically in
the last 50 years.

5 In order to live well after you retire, you should begin saving as early as possible.
Experts suggest that after you stop working, you will need 70 to 75 percent of
your **salary** to live on every month. In other words, if you make $3,000 per month
while working, you will need between $2,100 and $2,250 per month to live on
45 during retirement. This calculation assumes that you have no mortgage[2] on a
house to continue paying, or other major expenses like your children's university
education. However, more retired people now rent their housing because they
can't afford to buy a home, so they will pay more in housing costs over time.
People also have to spend more on health care because they live longer; many
50 people in developed countries now live into their 80s or 90s.

6 Due to increased demand for housing, higher inflation, and a longer life
expectancy, a million dollars may not be enough to live on. Of course, where you
live and how long you live will influence how far a million dollars can go. To be
able to retire early, travel the world, and build your dream home, you may have to
55 be a millionaire many times over!

---

[2] A **mortgage** is a long-term loan given by banks to help people buy property.

Reading Comprehension
Check Your Understanding

A **Write the paragraph number (1–6) next to each main idea.**

_____ People need more savings in order to retire comfortably.

_____ A million dollars is not worth as much as people think.

_____ Many factors influence how far a million dollars can go.

_____ The cost of living has increased due to inflation.

_____ Property in city centers has become much more expensive.

_____ Property is more expensive because there is greater demand and less supply.

B **Read the following statements. Check (✓) whether they have gone up (▲) or down (▼) over the last 20 years.**

		▲	▼
1	the value of a million dollars		
2	average price of a house in the U.S.		
3	health care costs		
4	the cost of food and housing		
5	how much people save		
6	the number of elderly people		
7	proportion of retired people who own their homes		

Critical Thinking

C **Discuss the following questions with a partner.**

1 Are housing prices rising in your country? How has this affected you, your friends, or your parents? What effect does this have on society in general?

2 How do you think governments can help solve the problem of rising property prices and rising cost of living in general?

Vocabulary Comprehension

Definitions

A **Match the words in the box to the correct definitions. Write a–h. The words are from the passage.**

a in reality	b fulfill	c dense	d property
e investment	f inflation	g necessities	h salary

1 _____ to achieve a stated goal or promise
2 _____ something you buy because it may be worth more in the future
3 _____ things that one owns; one's house or land
4 _____ thick; close together
5 _____ actually; in fact
6 _____ money one is paid for working
7 _____ something everyone needs, e.g. food, clothing
8 _____ a continuing increase in prices over time

B **Complete the following sentences using the words from A. You might have to change the form of the word.**

1 Many people in developing countries do not have access to _____ such as food or clean water.
2 I rejected the job offer because the _____ offered is too low. It doesn't pay as well as my current job.
3 I had planned for this project to last three months, but _____ it took almost twice that time!
4 Make sure you can afford the mortgage if you decide to buy _____ .
5 The population is very _____ in Chinese cities like Shanghai and Beijing, as many people come from the countryside to find work.
6 The price of a movie ticket has nearly doubled in the last 20 years due to _____ .
7 She's looking for a job in New York so she can _____ her dream of living there.
8 The government funded the building of a football stadium as part of its long-term _____ in sports.

A Use *in-*, *il-*, *im-*, or *ir-* to complete the words below. Then discuss the meaning of each word with a partner.

1 There are still people in the United States who are _____literate—they can barely read or write.
2 It's quite _____probable that the thief climbed through the window when it's nearly 20 meters above the ground.
3 It is difficult to breathe on a mountain because there is _____sufficient oxygen in the air.
4 Sandra has an _____rational fear of the dark. She even has a night light by her bed.
5 Her handwriting was so _____legible that the teacher could not mark her test paper.
6 I won't ask John for advice in the future; what he told me was completely _____relevant to my situation
7 Cancer is still an _____curable disease.
8 After waiting for Maria for 20 minutes, Albert began to get _____patient.

B Complete the following sentences using the words in the box.

illogical   immature   inseparable   irresponsible   incapable

1 It was _____ of you to leave the door unlocked after going out.
2 Marco may be 30 years old, but he is very _____. He still behaves like a teenager.
3 Han is so self-absorbed that he seems _____ of thinking about anyone but himself.
4 I thought Cathy's explanation was completely _____. She didn't answer my question at all.
5 Atsushi and his brother are _____. They even signed up for the same classes at university.

In this chapter you read the word *impossible*. This word begins with the prefix *im-*, meaning *not* or *the opposite of*. The prefix *in-* can also mean *not*. When *in-* comes before the letter *l*, the prefix changes to *il-*. Before *m* or *p*, it changes to *im-*. Before *r*, it changes to *ir-*.

CHAPTER 2 Lottery Winners: Rich...but Happy?

Before You Read
Lottery Facts

A Look at the information below. Which of these statistics are surprising to you? What does this tell you about the chances of winning a lottery?

In our lifetime, what are the chances of ...	
...being born with 11 fingers or toes?	**1 in 500**
...drowning?	**1 in 1,008**
...living to 100 years old?	**1 in 6,000**
...finding a pearl in an oyster?	**1 in 12,000**
...getting struck by lightning?	1 in 280,000
...winning the Mega Millions Jackpot?	1 in 176,000,000

B Discuss the following questions with a partner.

1 Do you know how the lottery works?
2 Do you know anyone who has won the lottery or received a lot of money all at one time? What did they do with the money?

Reading Skill
Previewing

Previewing is something good readers do when they first encounter new reading material. They ask themselves questions like these: *What is this about? What kind of text is this?* and *What do I already know about it?* Previewing can involve skimming, scanning, and predicting to help us get acquainted with the reading passage.

A Take one minute to preview the passage on the pages 73–74. Think about the title and the picture, scan the passage for interesting information, and skim the first and last paragraphs.

B Now discuss the following questions with a partner.

1 What do you think the passage is about?
2 What do you already know about this subject?
3 What interesting points did you notice?
4 Where could you look to learn more about this topic?
5 Do you think you'll enjoy reading the passage?

C Read the entire passage carefully. Then answer the questions on page 75.

Lottery Winners: Rich...but Happy?

Every week, millions of dollars are spent, and won, on lottery tickets. With jackpots hitting hundreds of millions of dollars, many lottery winners suddenly find themselves with much more money than they're used to. Many will have enough to purchase a new car, buy a luxury house, take a holiday and quit working—all within
5 a short space of time. These "lucky" few, however, may end up with more problems than they had before they struck it rich. According to financial planner Steven Goldbart, two out of three winners spend all their winnings within five years.

Newly **affluent** lottery winners are actually in quite a **tricky** situation, so much so that lottery organizers employ counselors to help them. These counselors
10 encourage winners to get advice from financial experts, such as accountants, about how best to invest their earnings. The counselors also help winners to understand how their lives may change for the better—and possibly for the worse. Many lottery winners are **sensible** when managing their new wealth; some, however, do not use their money **wisely** and end up getting into various **unforeseen** difficulties. Take a
15 look at the fortunes of two very different lottery winners.

Michael Carroll is an example of what can happen to lottery winners if they don't manage their money carefully. When Carroll was 19 years
20 old, he won £10 million in England's National Lottery. At the time, Carroll was working as a garbage collector, and the money changed his life. Three months after winning the
25 lottery, he bought a home in a small town and turned the backyard into a 24-hour racetrack. The constant noise and dust upset his neighbors. He also purchased several luxury vehicles but was stopped for driving a brand new BMW without license plates or insurance. He was **banned** from driving for six months. This wasn't Carroll's first encounter with the law – he was frequently

30 arrested for drug possession and other crimes, and was jailed for nine months in 2006 for violent behavior. Upon his release from prison, Carroll applied for loans to make the payments on properties he had bought and to continue funding his **extravagant** lifestyle. In just eight years, Carroll had spent all his winnings. It was reported in 2010 that he was trying to get his old job as a
35 garbage collector back.

After winning almost $29 million in a North Carolina lottery in 2009, Billy and Jeff Wilson say they have learned a lot about managing money. When people found out that the father and son had won so much money, the family had to leave their hometown to avoid 40 people asking them for financial help. Billy, the elder Wilson, stopped working
45 but likes to believe that winning the lottery hasn't really changed them as people. He said: "We live around a bunch of millionaires and some of them are the most miserable people on Earth. Just because you have money doesn't make you any better than anyone else and sometimes it seems like they forgot that." His son Jeff says he just enjoys hanging out with friends and fishing.
50 Thanks to the sensible way in which they handled their lottery money, the Wilsons are set to enjoy their winnings for a long, long time.

If you should happen to be lucky enough to win a lottery, here are a few simple rules that financial advisors recommend following.

- Meet with an accountant or other financial advisor.
55 - Pay all **debts**, such as home mortgages, car loans, and credit card bills.
- Calculate how much money will be needed to live on every year and then invest the extra money.
- Hand in your resignation only when you know you really don't need the job anymore.

A Choose the correct answers for the following questions.

1 The word *lucky* (line 5) is in quotation marks because lottery winners _____.

   a depend on skill and not luck to win

   b may encounter problems with their money

   c will soon lose all their money

2 What do lottery counselors do?

   a They organize and run the lottery.

   b They help lottery winners make financial investments.

   c They help lottery winners cope with their sudden wealth.

3 The word *fortunes* in line 15 does NOT mean _____.

   a luck

   b money

   c outcome

4 According to the passage, what should lottery winners do?

   a Quit their jobs soon after winning.

   b Pay their credit card bills.

   c Invest all their lottery winnings.

5 What could be another title for the passage?

   a The Biggest Lottery Winners

   b Winning the Lottery: What Happens Next?

   c How to Hit the Jackpot

B Read the following sentences. Check (✓) whether they apply to Michael Carroll (C) and/or the Wilsons (W).

The lottery winner(s) . . .	C	W
1 stopped working.		
2 moved to a new place.		
3 got into trouble with the police.		
4 had to borrow money eventually.		
5 is/are still living on the prize money.		

C Discuss the following questions with a partner.

Critical Thinking

1 Do you think rich people are treated differently? How would people treat someone who has just won a lottery?

2 What personal qualities help a person to handle money well?

Motivational Tip: Share with others. Think of two ways that you can share what you learn from this chapter with people who are not in your class. Do you have a friend that you can email after class today? Tell him/her what you learned about the value of money today in your class. As you share what you read with others, your reading skills will improve.

Vocabulary Comprehension
Words in Context

A **Choose the best answer. The words in blue are from the passage.**

1 An affluent person has a lot of _____.
   a talent   **b** money

2 If a math problem is tricky, it _____.
   a doesn't have an obvious solution   **b** can be solved easily

3 A sensible person usually _____.
   a acts without thinking   **b** thinks before acting

4 Which is considered a wise investment?
   a taking a course on computer skills   **b** buying a candy bar

5 An unforeseen encounter is a meeting that you don't _____.
   a expect   **b** remember

6 If you are banned from something, you are _____.
   a not allowed to do it   **b** invited to do it

7 An example of an extravagant expense is _____.
   a a diamond cat collar   **b** a washing machine

8 A person who has a debt _____ money.
   a has saved   **b** owes

B **Answer the following questions, then discuss your answers with a partner. The words in blue are from the passage.**

1 Have you encountered any unforeseen difficulties in learning English?
2 What is the most extravagant thing you've ever bought?
3 What are some things that are banned in your classroom?
4 What do you think people mean when they refer to "sensible shoes"?
5 What is the wisest piece of advice that anyone has ever given you?
6 Why do you think more and more young people are in debt nowadays?
7 Which is the most affluent neighborhood in your city?
8 Have you ever been in a tricky situation involving a friend? Why was it tricky?

A Write the correct *-ent* or *-ant* word for each definition. Use the words in italics to help you. You may use a dictionary to help with spelling.

1 _____: a person who lives or *resides* in a certain place
2 _____: *pleasing* to you
3 _____: describes someone who challenges or *defies* authority
4 _____: to depend or *rely* on something or someone
5 _____: empty, having a *vacancy*, unoccupied
6 _____: someone who *participates* in something
7 _____: when something is obvious from *evidence*
8 _____: a person who makes a formal *application* for something, e.g. a job
9 _____: a person, plant, or animal that is *descended* from a particular ancestor
10 _____: open to and able to *tolerate* different views, beliefs, or behavior

Vocabulary Skill
The Suffixes *-ent* and *-ant*

In this chapter you read the word *affluent*, which ends with the suffix *-ent*, and *extravagant*, which ends with the suffix *-ant*. These suffixes can be used to form adjectives like in the passage. They can also be used to describe someone or something that performs a specific action (e.g. a *servant* is someone who *serves*).

B Complete the following sentences with the correct forms of the *-ent* or *-ant* words from A.

1 It was _____ that she had not prepared for the meeting as she had no idea what to say.
2 Nearly 12 percent of people in the United States are _____ of Irish settlers who came to North America over the centuries.
3 A(n) _____ society is one that is accepting of all races and religions.
4 The _____ of the building were unhappy with the noise caused by the construction next door.
5 The position is still _____ because we haven't found a suitable person for the job.
6 There's a(n) _____ smell coming from the refrigerator. I hope the food hasn't gone rotten.
7 He has been getting into trouble at school for starting fights and being openly _____ toward teachers.
8 Nowadays, people are so _____ on technology to keep in touch with friends.

C Think of two more words that end with *-ent* or *-ant*. Write a definition for each and see whether your partner can guess the words.

Real Life Skill

Understanding Money and Banking Terms

If you're planning a trip to an English-speaking country, it is often helpful to learn about local banking customs and practices. Becoming familiar with some of the common money and banking terms will help you to better enjoy your stay.

A The following are common words and phrases used in many English-speaking countries. Discuss their meanings with a partner.

Forms of payment	Using a bank machine	At the bank
cash	ATM[1]	open a checking account
check	PIN[2]	currency exchange
debit card	withdraw	money transfer
credit card	deposit	deposit

[1]Automated Teller Machine   [2]Personal Identification Number

B Complete the sentences below using words and phrases from A.

1 You will need a(n) _____ if you want to reserve a hotel room via the Internet.

2 If you want to send or receive money electronically, you should visit a bank or a credit agency and ask about doing a(n) _____.

3 You have Euros, but you need American dollars. You should visit a place that does _____.

4 You have $500 in your checking account. You go to a(n) _____ and _____ $85. Your balance is now $415.

C Below is a common form of payment in the United States. What is it? Imagine you need to pay $120.50 to Kean's Department Store. Complete the missing information.

222 Shannon Street,
San Francisco, CA 94134   Date _____   811

Pay to the order of _____ $ _____

_____ DOLLARS

Bank of America
1234 001 234 567   _____

What do you think?

1 What are some ways that you can guard your money against inflation?
2 Why do you think people play the lottery if the chances of winning are so low?
3 Can you name any famous billionaires? How did they get their wealth?
4 Do you think wealthy people should donate money to charity? Why, or why not?

Celebrations Around the World

Getting Ready

Discuss the following questions with a partner.

1 What is happening in the pictures above? What events are they celebrating?
2 How do people in your country or culture celebrate these events?
3 What is your favorite cultural celebration? Explain your answer.

Before You Read
Wedding Quiz

A Answer the following questions about weddings.

1 The word *bride* comes from the Old English word for _____.
   a wife   b love   c cook

2 In European cultures, the man traditionally proposes to the woman

   _____.

   a on both knees   b on one knee   c standing up

3 The custom of having a best man began in Germany. He originally

   helped the groom _____.
   a buy the wedding ring and get dressed
   b choose a bride from women in the village
   c capture his bride from another village

4 Which metal is traditionally very important in Indian weddings?
   a gold   b silver   c bronze

5 Which of these expressions means "to get married"?
   a tie the knot   b kick the bucket   c buy the farm

**B Discuss your answers with a partner. Then check your answers at the
bottom of page 81.**

Reading Skill
Using Subheadings to
Predict Content

Sometimes reading
passages are divided
into paragraphs or
sections that have
subheadings. We
can use our existing
knowledge of the topic
and these subheadings
to predict some of the
ideas that may be in
the reading.

**A Look at the article on the pages 81–82. Read only the title and the four
subheadings. Fill in the chart below with your predictions on what will
be in each paragraph.**

Subheading	Ideas
The Wedding Dress	
The Rings	
Flowers	
Gifts	

**B Skim each of the four main paragraphs. Are any of your ideas in the
chart the same as the ideas in the article?**

**C Now read the entire passage carefully. Then answer the questions on
page 83.**

Wedding Customs

Marriage is a part of nearly every culture in the world, but marriage traditions vary greatly from place to place.

The Wedding Dress

5 In many countries, it is **customary** for the bride to wear a white dress as a symbol of her innocence. The tradition of wearing a special white dress for the wedding ceremony started over 150 years ago in 1840, when Queen Victoria married in white. Before that, brides wore all sorts

10 of colors (even black!) and most could not **afford** to buy a dress that they would only wear once. Modern brides are more fortunate: dresses are still white but are now available in a variety of styles and **fabrics**. Many women even have their dresses specially designed and tailored. Not all cultures celebrate with white, however. In certain Asian countries and in the Middle East, red and orange are

15 considered symbols of joy and happiness. In Asia it is not uncommon for the bride and groom to change clothes several times as the ceremony progresses.

The Rings

In many cultures, couples exchange rings, usually made of gold or silver, during the marriage ceremony. The circular shape of the ring is symbolic of the couple's

20 **eternal** union. In Brazil, it is traditional to have the rings **engraved** with the bride's name on the groom's ring and **vice versa**. In the United States, England, Canada, and France, the wedding ring is usually worn on the third finger of the left hand because it was once believed that a vein

25 ran directly from this finger to the heart. But wedding and engagement rings aren't always jewelry for the fingers. In traditional Hindu relationships, the man gives the woman a *bichiya*—a ring worn on the toe—as a symbol

30 of their engagement.

The groom puts a *bichiya* on the bride's foot, which is decorated with henna (a natural and temporary dye).

Answers to Wedding Quiz (page 80): 1. c 2. b 3. c 4. a 5. a

Flowers

Flowers play an important role in most weddings. Roses are said to be the flowers of love, and because roses usually bloom in June (in the
35 Northern Hemisphere[1]), this has become the most popular month for weddings in many countries. Ivy is also used in wedding bouquets because in early Greek times it was thought to be a sign of everlasting love. The flower bouquets of some
40 Middle Eastern brides contain Artemisia—a bitter herb—to symbolize that the marriage will survive

A bride prepares to toss her wedding bouquet to the waiting crowd.

both good times and bad. In Thai weddings, the mothers of the bride and groom lay flowers on the shoulders of the couple to bring happiness and luck to their marriage. Flower garlands[2] are also exchanged in addition to rings to represent
45 the beauty of marriage and life. After the wedding ceremony, it is customary in many countries for the bride to throw her bouquet into a crowd of well-wishers, usually her single female friends. It is said that the person who catches the bouquet will be the next one to marry.

Gifts

50 In Chinese cultures, wedding guests give gifts of money to the newlyweds in small red envelopes. Money is also an **appropriate** gift at Korean and Japanese weddings. Not all cultures, however, give money. In many Western countries such as the United Kingdom, wedding guests give the bride and groom household items that they may need for their new home. In Russia, rather than receiving gifts,
55 the bride and groom provide gifts to their guests instead. In Scotland, a week before the wedding ceremony, the bride's mother may invite the guests to her house and show off all the wedding gifts received, unwrapped, each with a card that has the giver's name on it.

Today, many couples choose to **integrate** wedding traditions from different
60 cultures around the world. With so many interesting practices to choose from, people can create the perfect occasion on their most special day.

---

[1] The **Northern Hemisphere** refers to the half of Earth that is north of the equator. North America and Europe are in this area.
[2] A **garland** is a string of flowers and leaves usually worn on the head or hung as decoration.

A **Choose the correct answer for the following questions.**

1 What changed soon after Queen Victoria's wedding?
a Women could buy wedding dresses in different fabrics.
b Women started wearing white wedding dresses.
c Women had their wedding dresses specially designed.

2 In most cultures, what does the wedding ring usually symbolize?
a joy and happiness
b wealth and luck
c everlasting love

3 In which culture do the bride and groom wear flowers on their shoulders?
a Greek
b Thai
c Middle Eastern

4 According to the passage, how are wedding traditions practiced nowadays?
a People pick and choose which traditions to use.
b People don't follow traditions anymore.
c People only follow the traditions of their own culture.

B **Answer the following questions with information from the passage.**

1 Why is the wedding ring worn on the third finger in some cultures?

_____

_____

2 Why is June a popular month for weddings to be held?

_____

_____

3 According to the passage, what happens to the single person who catches the bride's bouquet?

_____

_____

4 What is the difference between Asian and Western cultures when it comes to giving wedding gifts?

_____

_____

C **Discuss the following questions with a partner.**

Critical Thinking

1 What are some popular wedding customs in your country? What is the significance of these customs?

2 Do you think society places a lot of importance on marriage? How do younger generations view marriage, compared to older generations?

Vocabulary Comprehension
Odd Word Out

A (Circle) the word or phrase that does not belong in each group. The words in blue are from the passage.

1	integrate	encounter	meet	bump into
2	written	engraved	printed	conducted
3	everlasting	extreme	eternal	unending
4	shorts	jacket	skirt	fabric
5	customary	normal	crazy	traditional
6	afford	drive	spend	buy
7	vice versa	opposite	different	regular
8	impressive	appropriate	dramatic	powerful

B Complete the following sentences with the words in blue from **A**. You might have to change the form of the word.

1 I really like that handbag but I can't _____ it.

2 Many religions have a concept of _____ life after death.

3 You have to dress _____ when attending a formal event like a wedding.

4 People used to believe that the sun went around the Earth, instead of _____ .

5 The government encourages immigrants to _____ with local people.

6 This necklace has my name _____ on it.

7 It's _____ in many Asian cultures to greet the oldest or most senior person first.

8 When you buy sportswear, be sure to get clothes with light and comfortable _____ .

Motivational Tip: What do others say about reading? Have you seen anything recently in a newspaper or a magazine about the importance of good English? Who made the statement? Try to be aware of what leaders in your country say about the importance of English skills, which include reading. Part of many countries' development goals is to improve the reading skills of their population. How can you support those goals?

A Complete the chart with the noun, verb, and adjective forms of words you've seen in this chapter. Not every word will have all three. Look again at the reading to find related words, or use a dictionary to help you.

Vocabulary Skill
Word Families

When you learn a new word in English, it is helpful to learn words that are related to it. Learning the different parts of speech that form the word family can help you expand your vocabulary.

	Noun	Verb	Adjective
1	symbol		
2			decorative
3	custom		
4		progress	
5	choice		
6			integrated
7			popular

B Complete the following paragraph using the correct words from the chart in **A**. You might have to change the form of the word.

Wedding Symbols and Superstitions

What will bring good luck to the bride and groom on their wedding day? Different cultures have different beliefs, but nearly all do something to wish the couple a long and happy marriage. In Italy, it's **(1)** _____ for the wedding guests to tie a ribbon in front of the building where the couple will marry. This is a **(2)** _____ of the couple's bond of marriage. There is another tradition in which the bride gives guests "confetti," which can be in the form of rice, paper, nuts, or candy-covered almonds. This represents fertility or the ability to have children. In Korea, ducks and geese are seen as faithful animals because they stay together for life, so people try to **(3)** _____ them into celebrations in some way. Many years ago, the groom would often give the bride's family a pair of geese; a modern Korean wedding ceremony may include **(4)** _____ such as hand-painted ducks. These are a **(5)** _____ of the couple's promise to stay together. In Japan, an old tradition is for the bride to be completely painted white, wearing a white kimono and heavy headpiece. However, many young couples **(6)** _____ not to continue this practice, so the **(7)** _____ of such traditions has declined.

CHAPTER 2 Travel Diary:
Yanshuei Fireworks Festival

Before You Read
Holiday Traditions

A Match the festivals in the box to the correct tradition. Write a–d.

> **a** Cinco de Mayo   **b** Ramadan   **c** Diwali   **d** Chinese New Year

1 _____ Mariachi bands play folk music at big celebrations.
2 _____ People give red envelopes with money in them.
3 _____ People fast (don't eat) from morning until night for one month.
4 _____ Little oil lamps are lit and placed around the house for up
to five days.

B Discuss your answers in **A** with a partner, then answer the following
questions.

1 Which countries celebrate the festivals above? Do you celebrate any of
them?
2 What traditions are unique to celebrations in your country?

Reading Skill
Recognizing Sequence of
Events

In reading passages
which feature a
personal account
or story, events are
usually organized
sequentially, in
the order that they
happened, or as the
writer experienced it.
It is very important for
us to understand which
events come first,
second, etc. Words like
when, later, now can
help you recognize the
sequence of events.

A Read the following sentences from the passage on the pages 87–88.
Without reading the passage, put the events in order from 1–6. Discuss
your ideas with a partner.

	I suddenly realized that I needed the extra clothes, gloves, and helmet to protect myself from the fireworks!
	Moments later, rockets were screaming, booming, and popping in all directions.
	When we got home we left our clothes outside because they smelled of smoke.
1	Last night my old roommate Lin invited me to a fireworks festival in the city of Yanshuei.
	When we arrived in Yanshuei we saw many preparations being made for the festival.
	I was surprised when Lin gave me an old sweatshirt, gloves, a towel, and a motorcycle helmet.

B Circle the words in the sentences that helped you choose the order.
Then skim the passage to check whether your answers in **A** are correct.

C Read the entire passage carefully. Then answer the questions on page 89.

Travel Diary: Yanshuei Fireworks Festival

By Michael Liu

I just returned from the most amazing experience of my life at the Yanshuei Fireworks Festival!

After spending some time with family in Taipei celebrating Chinese New Year, I'm staying the weekend with friends in Tainan, in the south of Taiwan. Last night my old
5 roommate Lin invited me to a fireworks festival in the city of Yanshuei. Since we were going to a fireworks festival, I assumed that I should pack a blanket and maybe some snacks for a picnic while we watched the fireworks. Naturally, I was surprised when Lin gave me an old sweatshirt, gloves, a towel, and a motorcycle helmet. When I asked why I needed these old clothes he smiled and said, "You'll see."

10 According to **legend**, in the 17th century a terrible plague[1] had been making the people of Yanshuei ill for years and no one could find a cure. When some citizens suggested that perhaps there were evil spirits in the town, the people decided to ask the war god, Guan Yu, to come and **drive away** the evil spirits. The people impressed Guan Yu with a huge fireworks display and **in return,** he drove out the spirits that had been plaguing
15 the town. Today the fireworks festival is an annual event to honor and thank Guan Yu.

When we arrived in Yanshuei, we saw many preparations being made for the festival, which starts after sunset and goes on all night. Near the center of town, we were greeted by the sight of large walls with many holes and open boxes facing in all directions. Lin told me that the local word for these walls means "beehive," and that they would be filled with
20 fireworks for the celebration. I suddenly realized that I needed the extra clothes, gloves, and helmet to protect myself from the fireworks! I looked around and noticed workers **stuffing** the beehives with fireworks of all kinds. Lin could see what I was thinking and he said that many people are injured by fireworks at this festival every year. I soon saw that

---

[1] A **plague** is a serious disease that spreads easily.

a few participants wear very little protection from the fireworks and receive many burns to the skin. 25

Nevertheless, we went to main site where the fireworks would be lit. A group of people were **worshipping** a statue of Guan Yu in front of a small beehive. After they sang a prayer, they 30 took the statue away and the crowd pushed forward. Lin said, "Put on your helmet and hop up and down a little when it starts." His advice was confusing, but when a man started to light the beehive everyone started hopping, so I joined in. 35

Moments later, rockets were screaming, booming, and popping in all directions. Fireworks **collided** with my helmet and bounced off my body. I closed my eyes and all I could smell was smoke from the **explosions**. It was over in a few seconds, but it felt much longer. I realized that the hopping was to shake off any fireworks that might get stuck and burn

40 you. My heart was racing[2] and I could feel a big smile on my face as I caught my breath and brushed myself off. That beehive was the first of many and each one seemed more amazing than the last.

45 Now I understood the name "beehive"— the sound of the fireworks became a constant buzzing in my ears.

When we got home we changed and left our clothes outside because they 50 smelled of smoke. Each of us had small burns and cuts from being hit with so many fireworks, but as we sat around the table eating a late dinner, we all felt we'd just had a great adventure.

[2] When your heart **races**, it beats very fast.

A Read the following sentences. Check (✓) whether they are true (T) or false (F).

		T	F
1	Michael and Lin are old friends.		
2	Michael was expecting a pleasant time watching fireworks.		
3	Guan Yu was an evil spirit that plagued Yanshuei.		
4	People say prayers before the fireworks are lit.		
5	People hop up and down to avoid the fireworks on the ground.		
6	People are not allowed to attend the festival if they don't wear protective clothing.		
7	The explosions from the beehive only lasted a few seconds.		
8	Michael and Lin were not injured at all by the fireworks.		

B Answer the following questions with information from the passage.

1 How did Michael's idea of a fireworks festival differ from Lin's?

_____

_____

2 According to the legend, why did the people of Yanshuei need Guan Yu's help?

_____

_____

3 What are two reasons that the locals call the walls "beehives"?

_____

_____

4 Did Michael enjoy the festival? Why do you think so?

_____

_____

Critical Thinking

C Discuss the following questions with a partner.

1 Fireworks are an important part of many Chinese rituals and events. What do you think these fireworks symbolize?
2 Have you ever participated in a celebration or tradition that might be unsafe? Would you? Why, or why not?

Vocabulary Comprehension

Definitions

A **Match the words in the box to the correct definitions. Write a–h. The words are from the passage.**

a legend	**b** drive away	**c** in return	**d** stuff (*v.*)
e nevertheless	**f** worship	**g** collide	**h** explosion

1 _____ in exchange for
2 _____ to smash together
3 _____ to force to leave
4 _____ a violent burst of energy
5 _____ in contrast to
6 _____ an old and traditional story
7 _____ to put something inside something else
8 _____ to show respect to a god, for example, by praying

B **Complete the following sentences using the words from A. You might have to change the form of the word.**

1 I was in a hurry so I _____ my books in my bag.
2 The _____ of Atlantis involves a wealthy city that sank to the bottom of the ocean.
3 There was a small _____ when the student mixed the wrong chemicals together.
4 My boss gave me two extra days off _____ for my working overtime.
5 Even though the food at that restaurant is good, the service is bad enough to _____ customers.
6 People are required to be quiet in places of _____ as a sign of respect.
7 The driver lost control of the car and it _____ with a motorcycle.
8 It rained all morning. _____, we went ahead with our football match.

Motivational Moment: More than the definition. After completing this vocabulary comprehension exercise, think about what it means to truly know a word. You need to know more than the definition to really know and understand a word. You know the contexts in which this word will appear, and you know what other words will be used near this word. The challenge is to think about more than just the definition of a word in order to improve your vocabulary skills.

A Match the words on the left with their definitions. You may use a dictionary to help you.

Homophones		Definitions	
1	_____ hire	a	forbidden; prohibited
2	_____ higher	b	to do too much of something
3	_____ isle	c	a small island
4	_____ aisle	d	further up than before
5	_____ overdue	e	to give someone a job
6	_____ overdo	f	to fly or rise high in the air
7	_____ band	g	past an agreed certain date or time
8	_____ banned	h	a music group
9	_____ sore	i	painful
10	_____ soar	j	a space or passage between seats or shelves

Vocabulary Skill
Homophones

In this unit you read the words *sight* and *site*. These words sound exactly the same but have different meaning and spelling. These types of words are called *homophones*, and there are many in the English language.

B Complete the following sentences using the homophones from **A**.

1 Birds with the largest wingspan are normally able to _____ in the air for much longer.

2 When my dad got too busy with work, he had to _____ an assistant.

3 I forgot to pay the rent and now it's _____.

4 My legs are _____ from running in a marathon yesterday.

5 When I travel by air, I like to sit by the _____ and not the window.

6 My childhood dream was to play guitar in a rock _____.

7 I never work out at the gym for more than one hour. I don't want to _____ it.

8 From the ship, we could see a small _____ covered with trees.

9 Even though wages are rising, the cost of living is much _____ than before.

10 He's been _____ from entering the hotel as he caused so much trouble there last time.

C Write a homophone for each word in the chart below. Discuss your answers with a partner, then add one more to the chart.

Word	Homophone
night	
whether	
bare	
piece	

Real Life Skill
Accepting and Declining Invitations

People often send invitations to events by post, or nowadays by email. It is useful to know some of the words and phrases typically found in such invitations, especially when it refers to what you should be wearing or what time you should arrive. Certain expressions are also used to accept or decline invitations.

A Read the invitation below and answer the following questions.

> You're invited to Tom and Amy's engagement party!
>
> **The Blue Moon**
>
> 1453 South Mission Boulevard
>
> Saturday, May 17, 7 PM – late
>
> Cocktails and hors d'oeuvres will be served.
>
> **Dress code:** Smart casual
>
> **RSVP:** No later than May 1

1 Where is the party being held?
2 When should you arrive?
3 What will the food be like?
4 What kind of clothes should you wear? Give some examples.
5 Do you have to reply to let them know that you will attend the party?

B Read the two replies below. Who is going to the party? Who isn't? <u>Underline</u> the words and phrases that helped you decide.

May 1
Dear Tom and Amy,
Thanks for the invitation; the party sounds like a lot of fun. I'm afraid I won't be able to make it, though, as I'm going to be out of town that weekend. Congratulations on the wedding plans!
Toshi

April 25
Tom and Amy,
Thanks for inviting us to your party. Mark and I will definitely be there to celebrate with you. Looking forward to seeing both of you!
Rita

C Using the expressions you've learned and others that you know, write a reply accepting or declining Tom and Amy's invitation.

What do you think?

1 Describe your ideal wedding. What would it be like? Who would you invite? Where would it be held?
2 Have there been any interesting celebrity weddings lately? Which ones caught your attention?
3 Many cultures celebrate events based on myths and legends. Can you think of any? Why would people celebrate something that might not be true or real?

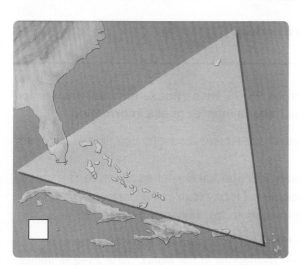

Getting Ready

Discuss the following questions with a partner.

1 Which mystery below does each picture show? Write a–d.

a crop circles   b the Loch Ness monster   c Bigfoot   d the Bermuda triangle

2 How would you explain each of these mysteries?

3 Do you believe there is a natural or logical explanation for these mysteries? Why, or why not?

CHAPTER 1 The "Lost World" of South America

Before You Read
Mount Mabu

In 2005, scientists using Google Earth (an online map) found a new forest on top of the little-known Mount Mabu in Mozambique, Africa. It was unknown to the rest of the world and didn't even appear on local maps. When they explored the forest in 2008, they found hundreds of new or rare species of wildlife. It turned out villagers in the area had kept the forest a secret so they could hide there in times of war.

A Read the information above, then answer the following questions.

1 Do you think there are still places in the world humans have yet to discover or fully explore? Why, or why not?
2 Would you want to visit such places? Why, or why not?

B Discuss your answers with a partner.

Reading Skill
Making Inferences

Information in a reading passage can be found in two ways: by what is stated directly and clearly on the page, or by what we can infer. When we infer, we use the existing information to draw conclusions about events, or the writer's opinion or purpose. It is a useful skill to know when reading and can help you better understand passages at a deeper level.

A Skim the passage on the pages 95–96, then choose the best answer for the following questions. You have to infer or guess information.

1 *The world is far less a mystery than it was a century ago* (line 1) suggests that _____ .
   a people are not so interested in natural mysteries anymore
   b the world is better understood today than in the past
   c the world is more of a mystery today than ever before

2 *"A few people have been there, but really not a lot, considering what they are—among the oldest formations in the world."* (line 21–23). Jesus Rivas, a biology professor, seems to think _____ .
   a there are too many tourists at the tepuis
   b people aren't allowed to visit tepuis because they are very old
   c not many people have actually visited the tepuis

3 Angel Falls is mentioned in paragraph 6 because it _____ .
   a is the only place you can visit in that region
   b shows how interesting the tepuis region is
   c shows how hard-to-reach the tepuis are

B Discuss your answers with a partner. Which lines in the passage helped you find the answer?

C Read the entire passage carefully. Then answer the questions on page 97.

The "Lost World" of South America

1 The world is far less a mystery than it was a century ago, but it still holds a few locations that **baffle** scientists and researchers. Early explorers spoke of mysterious mountains towering above South America's jungle. Such stories inspired Arthur Conan Doyle to write *The Lost World*, a novel set in an isolated
5 place still inhabited by dinosaurs. The dinosaurs were **fiction** ... but the mountains are real.

2 The mountains are called *tepuis*, or "house of the gods," in the language of the local Pémon. Rising thousands of meters into the
10 sky over the jungles of Guyana, Brazil, and Venezuela, these are dramatic sandstone structures (called *mesas* by geologists) with flat tops and steep sides. Tepuis are so **remote** that they have prevented researchers
15 from exploring them fully—they truly are among the last unexplored places on Earth.

Mount Roraima, one of the tepuis

3 The flat **summits**, ranging from a few square kilometers to dozens and even hundreds of square kilometers, used to be connected. Some scientists even believe that these tepuis have life forms from the ancient super continent[1]
20 known as Gondwana, which may have included what we know today as South America, Africa, Antarctica, Australia, and other land masses. "A few people have been there, but really not a lot, considering what they are—among the oldest formations in the world," Jesus Rivas, a biology professor, said. "They are like a place where time stopped. In the fauna[2] you can see South America evolving for
25 the last 300 million years."

4 The high **altitude** and the ancient age of the tepuis make them extremely interesting to biologists. They are frequently described as "islands in the sky,"

---

[1] A **super continent** is one giant landmass formed from several different continents coming together through natural forces.
[2] **Fauna** refers to the animals of a particular region, habitat, or time period.

Angel Falls

covered in tropical greenery that supports a wide range of wildlife. Indeed, many of the species that live on top
30 of the tepuis are found nowhere else on the planet. But because they are so hard to reach, scientists have only begun to scratch the surface of the enormous diversity on and around the tepuis.

5 One question still mystifies scientists: how did animals
35 and plants end up in such an **inaccessible** place? Some scientists believe in the "Lost World" theory—that these creatures have been living there since the tepuis were born. But, in a paper published in the journal *Evolution*, studies on tree frogs exclusive to these tepuis showed that they had climbed up
40 slowly over a few million years. Unfortunately, until further studies are conducted, scientists can only **speculate**.

6 People who want to visit these tepuis can arrange special tours, but it will require enormous effort to get there. To make a comparison, Angel Falls in Venezuela— the tallest waterfall in the world—is probably the most popular tourist destination
45 in the tepui region. However, the base of the falls can only be reached after flying into the jungle and hiking for hours.

a scene from the animated film
***Up*, showing the tepuis**

7 When the creators of *Up* (a movie which featured the tepuis) visited to get a feel of the place, they chose Roraima—
50 the "easiest" of the tepuis to climb. Bob Peterson, one of the climbers, said: "It was like your worst nightmare. It was like a six- or seven-hour climb to the top, and I had on way too much gear. When we got
55 to the top, we had to hike across uneven **terrain** for another hour and a half. It was already dark when we got to our camp. And suddenly, from out of the darkness we saw this cave lit by candles and there was warm soup waiting for us. When we saw our tents, most of us just sat down and started crying. We were so happy to be there."

A Choose the correct answers for the following questions.

1 Why is there still not much known about the tepuis?
   a They were discovered only very recently.
   b They are too remote for people to explore.
   c They are restricted and protected by the locals.
2 According to the passage, which is true about Gondwana?
   a It has broken up into other smaller continents.
   b Scientists believe the wildlife that lived there has gone extinct.
   c It was about the same size as continents like South America and Africa.
3 Tepuis are described as "islands in the sky" because, like islands, they _____.
   a are very isolated
   b were formed by volcanoes
   c are surrounded by water
4 Which is probably NOT true about the life forms on the tepuis?
   a Some originated from the base of the tepuis.
   b They have been studied thoroughly by scientists.
   c They are unlike plants and animals elsewhere.
5 What is the main idea of paragraph 5?
   a There are many unique species of tree frogs living on the tepuis.
   b One of the theories about its wildlife is based on the book *The Lost World*.
   c Scientists are still unsure as to how wildlife ended up on the tepuis.

B Answer the following questions using information from the passage.

1 What about the tepuis might have inspired Arthur Conan Doyle to write *The Lost World*?

   _____

   _____.

2 What are "mesas"?

   _____

   _____.

3 Why are biologists so interested in the wildlife on the tepuis?

   _____

   _____.

4 Why did Bob Peterson and his crew cry when they reached their camp on top of Roraima?

   _____

   _____.

C Discuss the following questions with a partner.

Critical Thinking

1 Do you think inaccessible places like Roraima should be made easier for tourists to visit? Why, or why not?
2 What kinds of things might scientists learn from studying unexplored places?

Vocabulary Comprehension
Words in Context

A **Choose the best answer. The words in blue are from the passage.**

1 A fictional story _____.
   a actually happened
   b is made up

2 Which is more remote?
   a an apartment in the city
   b a tent in the desert

3 What does it mean to be at the summit of one's career?
   a You are at your most successful.
   b You have only just started out.

4 You can use altitude to measure _____.
   a how high an airplane flies in the sky
   b how tall a basketball player is

5 A baffling illness is _____ for doctors to treat.
   a easy
   b difficult

6 What would cause a place to be more inaccessible?
   a A new highway is built to reach it.
   b The only bridge to it is destroyed.

7 Students are likely to learn about terrain in _____ class.
   a history
   b geography

8 If people speculate that the price of oil will rise, they _____.
   a think it might rise
   b are sure it will rise

B **Answer the following questions, then discuss your answers with a partner. The words in blue are from the passage.**

1 Do you select a place to live based on how accessible it is?
2 What are some genres of fiction?
3 Give an example of a remote place.
4 Is there anything about the English language that baffles you?
5 What kind of shoe is appropriate for rough terrain?
6 Can you name the world's highest summit?
7 Do you think stock market speculation is dangerous? Why, or why not?
8 What else can altitude be used to measure?

A Here are some common prefixes used with the root *spec/spect*. Match the prefix with its correct meaning. You may use your dictionary to help you.

1 _____ ex-   **a** below, under
2 _____ in-   **b** forward
3 _____ intro-   **c** out, away
4 _____ pro-   **d** back, backward
5 _____ retro-   **e** within
6 _____ sus-   **f** into

B Complete the following sentences with the correct word from the box.

(expect   suspect   inspect   prospective   introspective   retrospect)

1 The police _____ Angela stole the money, but they can't prove it.
2 We _____ the plane will arrive on time; it's scheduled to come in at 3:00 this afternoon.
3 Ricardo got married at age 20, but in _____, he thinks he should have waited until he was older.
4 Carmen has two _____ buyers for her paintings. She feels certain that at least one will purchase some of her work.
5 Her _____ essay about the death of her mother touched me greatly.
6 When I arrived in London, the customs officials opened my bags to _____ the contents.

C Think of two more words using *spec*, *spect*, or *spic*. Write a sentence for each. You may use your dictionary to help you.

Vocabulary Skill
The Root Word *spec* + Prefixes

In this unit you learned the word *speculation*, meaning *guessing about something*. This word begins with the root word *spec* meaning *to observe* or *to watch*, and is combined with the noun suffix *-tion*, meaning *the act of*. Spec, spect, and *spic* are combined with prefixes and suffixes to form many words in English. When it is used with some prefixes such as *ex-*, the spelling of the word changes.

Motivational Tip: Setting goals. Set a goal for your own personal reading rate on the next passage (refer to the Reading Rate chart on page 240). When we set a goal, we have something to work toward. The goal must be realistic but challenging. When you work toward and achieve your reading rate goals, you will feel a great sense of satisfaction.

CHAPTER 2 Is "Spontaneous Human Combustion" Possible?

Before You Read
Do You Believe It?

A **Read the following sentences. Which ones do you believe?**

1 Some people are able to move things using their minds.
2 Some people are able to see or communicate with dead people.
3 Earth is frequently visited by beings from other worlds.
4 If you talk to your plants and play soft music for them, they will grow faster.
5 Ancient civilizations have been able to predict things that happen many years in the future.

B **Discuss your answers in A with a partner, then answer the following questions.**

1 Can you think of any unusual events that have happened in your country or around the world?
2 Do you think there are some things that science cannot explain? Why, or why not?

Reading Skill
Identifying Main Ideas within Paragraphs

To guess the meaning of an important but unfamiliar word in a reading passage, try the following: First, think about how the new word is related to the topic of the reading. Second, identify what part of speech it is. Then look at the words surrounding the new word for synonyms, antonyms, or an explanation of the word.

A **Read the following sentences from the passage on the next page. Then answer the questions about the words in bold.**

This scene describes a typical case of **spontaneous human combustion** (SHC), in which a human body is supposedly able to burst into flames and to burn to almost nothing entirely on its own—that is, without an external cause. In most SHC cases, there are no witnesses to see how the person caught fire. In rare cases, the observer, who is often a friend or family member, tries to put out the fire. Occasionally the victim survives. Again, there is no clear outside cause—the blaze appears to start from within the victim's own body.

1 The word *spontaneous* is a(n) (verb / noun / adjective).
2 In this sentence, *spontaneous* probably means _____ .
   a accidental **b** forced **c** self-generated
3 The word *combustion* is a(n) (verb / noun / adjective)
4 In this sentence, *combustion* probably means _____ .
   a burning **b** accident **c** mystery

B Underline the sentences in the paragraph that helped you find the answers in **A**. Then discuss your answers with a partner.

C Now read the entire passage carefully. Then answer the questions on page 103.

Is "Spontaneous Human Combustion" Possible?

1 It happens something like this. Someone finds a badly burnt body in a poorly **ventilated** room. The body is sitting in a chair or lying on a bed or the floor. The
5 upper body of the **victim** is a heap of ashes, but one or more mostly undamaged hands or feet may be visible as well. A layer of blackened grease covers the ceiling and walls above the victim's head, but fire
10 damage in the room is limited to a small area right around and above the body. Objects only a meter away remain untouched by the blaze. Police investigators find no obvious source or cause for the fire.

the remains of an SHC victim

2 This scene describes a typical case of **spontaneous** human combustion (SHC), in which a human body is **supposedly** able to burst into flames and to burn to
15 almost nothing entirely on its own. In most SHC cases, there are no witnesses to see how the person caught fire. In rare cases, the observer, who is often a friend or family member, tries to put out the fire. Occasionally the victim survives. Again, there is no clear outside cause—the blaze appears to start from within the victim's own body.

3 20 This phenomenon is actually nothing new. A 1763 book by Frenchman Jonas Dupont with the title *De Incendiis Corporis Humani Spontaneis* describes in detail a
25 number of cases of SHC. A century later, Charles Dickens used SHC to kill off one of the characters in his novel *Bleak House*. A number of more recent unexplained deaths have
30 helped to keep the theory of SHC alive. One of the latest cases was of Michael Faherty, a 76-year-old man who was found burned to death in his home in Galway, Ireland, on

Krook dies of SHC in the novel *Bleak House*.

35 22 December 2010. Police arrived to find mostly ashes, with his head near an empty fireplace. The room was undamaged by the fire. After a **thorough** investigation, the coroner recorded Mr. Flaherty's death as a case of "spontaneous human combustion."

4 People have tried to explain these
40 mysterious deaths in various ways. Some have said that SHC can be set off by a build-up of electricity or gases within the body. The most reasonable explanation seems to be the "wick" or
45 "candle" theory. This says that, under certain circumstances, the human body can **function** as sort of an inside-out candle. That is, the fabric in a person's

The "wick" theory is one of the explanations for SHC.

clothing acts like the wick, and the fat in a person's body like the wax in the
50 candle. A spark from a nearby source could set off a small fire and the burning clothes would cause a person's body fat to melt, adding fuel to the fire. In a poorly ventilated room, the body can burn for hours and cause the kind of damage seen in many of the supposed SHC cases. In this **scenario,** the combustion is not "spontaneous" at all and is always caused by some **external** fire source.

5 55 In a recent experiment, the criminologist Dr. John de Haan put the wick theory to the test. De Haan wrapped a dead pig (chosen because the body fat of a pig is similar to that of a human) in a blanket, poured gasoline over it, set it on fire and then let it burn in a badly ventilated room. After burning for several hours, the body of the pig was reduced to ashes, much like the bodies of many supposed SHC victims.

6 60 De Haan's experiment did not persuade everyone that the wick theory explains SHC. Some believe there are still too many unanswered questions in many of the cases. What about the situations where no external source of the fire was found or where victims have burst into flame in front of witnesses? Until scientists come up with a theory that explains all of these circumstances, many will likely continue to
65 believe in the possibility of spontaneous human combustion.

A **Choose the correct answers for the following questions.**

1 The purpose of the first paragraph is probably NOT to _____ .
   a explain the concept of SHC
   b show why people still believe in SHC
   c give an example of how an SHC scene would look

2 Who used the idea of SHC to kill off a fictional character?
   a Charles Dickens
   b Jonas Dupont
   c Dr. John de Haan

3 What is the main idea of paragraph 3?
   a SHC has been mentioned in many works of fiction.
   b People still do not know the reason behind SHC.
   c There have been cases of SHC over the centuries.

4 According to the "wick" theory, what fuels an SHC fire?
   a body fat   b electricity   c gases

5 In which scenario is the "wick" theory of SHC most likely to occur?
   a A person has closed the windows and is sitting next to a fireplace.
   b A person has just undressed and is getting ready to shower.
   c A person is sleeping by an open window with a box of matches in his pocket.

6 The author probably wrote this article to _____ .
   a convince people that SHC is true
   b warn people that SHC can happen to them
   c explain SHC and relate its history

B **Read the following sentences. Check (✓) whether they are true (T) or false (F).**

		T	F
1	Victims of spontaneous human combustion always die.		
2	The police only found Michael Faherty's ashes when they arrived.		
3	A well ventilated room will probably prevent SHC from occuring.		
4	John de Haan used a pig in his experiment because its body fat is like a human's.		
5	John de Haan's theory explains how SHC can occur even without an external source.		

C **Discuss the following questions with a partner.**

Critical Thinking

1 Do you believe in spontaneous human combustion? Why, or why not?
2 Do you think there is any way to prove whether SHC is actually true?

Vocabulary Comprehension
Odd Word Out

A (Circle) the word or phrase that does not belong in each group. The words in blue are from the passage.

1	thorough	detailed	full	limited
2	extravagant	external	outer	exterior
3	examine	analyze	function	explain
4	misfortune	accident	scenario	failure
5	eternal	spontaneous	unplanned	sudden
6	seemingly	intentionally	supposedly	apparently
7	limited	airy	fresh	ventilated
8	victim	signal	indication	sign

B Complete the following sentences using the words in blue from **A**. You might have to change the form of the word.

1 James Bond has a custom-made watch that also _____ as a compass.

2 Gina has a reputation for being _____. She does what she wants, when she wants, without warning.

3 The police conducted a(n) _____ investigation of the murder scene but couldn't find fingerprints.

4 When painting the interior of a house, make sure the area is well _____.

5 Job applicants should display leadership skills and the ability to respond to real-world business _____.

6 The _____ of the attack told a different version of the story than his attacker.

7 A man in London has _____ witnessed a case of SHC, but I don't believe it.

8 The medication is for _____ use only, so please don't try and swallow it.

Motivational Tip: Reflect on your goals. Reflect back on the reading rate goal that you set for yourself before you started this chapter. Did you achieve your goal? Why, or why not? If you achieved your goal, find a way to celebrate! If you did not achieve your goal, determine what you need to do in the next unit to reach it.

A Look at the different kinds of collocations below.

Verb + Preposition: Some verbs can be used with certain prepositions.

> My big dictionary also *functions as* a doorstop.
> Jane *regarded* his *offer* to help with suspicion.

Adjective + Noun: Certain noun and adjective combinations work together to talk about one thing.

> Let's get some *fresh air.*
> He is my *close/good/best friend.*

Verb + Noun: Some nouns go with certain verbs to talk about one idea.

> Who is going *to make dinner?*
> When will you *go shopping?*

Vocabulary Skill
Collocations

In English, there are word pairs that naturally go together. In this chapter, for example, you learned the word *function.* This verb can stand alone, but in many sentences it is also used together with the preposition *as.* Becoming familiar with common word combinations can help you to better use and recall vocabulary you've learned.

B Match the words in the box with the nouns and prepositions below to form some common collocations. Some words will have more than one match. Use your dictionary to help you. Discuss your answers with a partner.

> make   do   go   hard   short   think   move   hope   know   work

1 _____ a decision
2 _____ with
3 _____ for
4 _____ about
5 _____ time

6 _____ on
7 _____ as
8 _____ of
9 _____ to
10 _____ work

C Complete the following paragraph with the correct noun, verb, adjective, or preposition. Be sure to use the correct form of the word. Check your answers with a partner.

Not many people know **(1)** _____ Alfred R. Riddle, the mystery hunter. When Alfred was very young, he **(2)** _____ a decision to dedicate his life to hunting mysteries. When he finished college, he moved **(3)** _____ Scotland for a **(4)** _____ time to look for the Loch Ness Monster. Later, he worked **(5)** _____ the U.S. government, searching the skies for UFOs. After that, he went **(6)** _____ Nepal, where he hoped **(7)** _____ discover the Yeti. He had a very **(8)** _____ time finding anything in all that snow, and Alfred never really liked **(9)** _____ work. Alfred decided to give up mystery hunting and now spends most of his time watching mystery programs on television.

Real Life Skill

Researching Mysteries Online

Being able to conduct Internet searches is an important skill. There is a wealth of information online about mysteries. Even if you can't understand all the writing on a website, your scanning skills can guide you to the information you want.

A Look at this list of mysterious places. Are any of them familiar to you? Choose three you would like to research online, or use your own ideas.

The Great Pyramid	The Sphinx	Baalbeck
Bermuda Triangle	Fatima	Atlantis
Machu Picchu	Chichen Itza	Kailasa Temple

B Search the Internet for information about the three places you chose in A. Complete the chart with the location and information about each place.

Mysterious place	Location	Interesting information

C Share the information you found with a partner.

What do you think?

1 Which of the mysteries you learned about in this unit is most intriguing to you? Why?
2 Do you know any mysteries that have been solved or have a scientific explanation behind them? Give an example.
3 What would the world be like if there weren't any mysteries in it?

Fluency Strategy: KWL

Readers can ask themselves three questions to improve their reading fluency and comprehension. The letters K, W, and L can be used to remind you of these questions. KWL stands for **K**now, **W**ant, **L**earn.

Know

The first step of KWL is similar to the Survey stage in SQ3R (page 161) and the A in the ACTIVE approach (inside front cover). This step will help you prepare yourself before reading.

A **The extract below is from the article on page 109. From the title and first paragraph, decide, "What is the topic of the passage?"**

America's Biggest Lottery Winner

One day in December 2002, Jack Whittaker decided to buy a lottery ticket at a small store in West Virginia. The 55-year-old didn't really need to as he was already a successful and affluent businessman. But Whittaker played the lottery that day because the prize was truly a fortune— $314 million. The next morning he learned he had won it all—the largest lottery win in the history of the United States at that time.

B Ask yourself, "What do I already know about this topic?" Write down three or four facts that you already know about the topic in the Know column of the table below.

Know	Want	Learn

Want

In the second stage of KWL, ask yourself, "What do I want to learn as I read?" By doing this you are reading with a purpose (see Review Unit 1).

A Ask yourself what you want to learn as you read *America's Biggest Lottery Winner*. Write down some things you hope to learn in the Want column above.

B Before going on to the next column, read the passage *America's Biggest Lottery Winner* on the next page.

America's Biggest Lottery Winner

Powerball jackpot winner Andrew "Jack" Whittaker (center right), his wife Jewell (center), granddaughter Brandi (center left), and daughter Ginger

1 One day in December 2002, Jack Whittaker decided to buy a lottery ticket at a small store in West Virginia. The 55-year-old didn't really need to as he was already a successful and affluent businessman. But Whittaker played the lottery that day because the prize was truly a fortune—$314 million. The next morning he learned he
5 had won it all—the largest lottery win in the history of the United States at that time.

2 Whittaker soon surprised everyone with his generosity. He bought property and a car for a worker at the store where he bought the winning ticket. He shared ten percent of his money with his church. He promised to set up a charitable organization to care for the poor of West Virginia. He seemed humble, saying he'd invest his money wisely and
10 continue to work at his company and "answer his own phone."

3 In reality, Whittaker was soon to experience the difficulties that tend to accompany a lottery win. People would wait for him to drop by his favorite store, and then they would beg him for money by telling him sad stories of illnesses and bad luck. Whittaker had to hire three people just to open letters asking him for money. "I don't have any friends," he said in a newspaper interview. "Every friend that I've had, practically, has wanted to borrow money or something and of course, once they borrow money from you, you can't be friends anymore."

4 It is also very hard to stay sensible when you have so much money. Whittaker reportedly grew extravagant and starting flashing his cash around. While drinking in a local club, he boasted of having $500,000 in cash in a briefcase in his car. He also started to make frequent trips to casinos for gambling, and witnesses said he became a troublemaker at these places, causing problems and growing angry when he was refused a request or banned from entering.

5

a flyer with a photo of Brandi posted near where her body was found

Whittaker loved his granddaughter, Brandi, immensely—he said that she was "his world." After winning, Whittaker treated his granddaughter to whatever she wanted; he bought her a new car and paid for her to meet the hip-hop star Nelly. According to Brandi's friend, she had a constant supply of money; it wasn't unusual for her to receive $5,000 in one day from her grandfather. With such money, her lifestyle gradually changed for the worse as she started to use illegal drugs with her friends. Her car was full of trash and money—there was so much of it that bills would occasionally fly out the window, according to another friend.

6 On December 4, 2003, Brandi disappeared. When they didn't hear from her over the next five days, the Whittakers called the police. Soon after, Brandi's body was found. She had died from an overdose[1] of illegal drugs.

7 Ten years on from winning the lottery, Jack Whittaker still struggles with health problems, his beloved wife has left him, and his precious granddaughter is gone. "If it would bring my granddaughter back, I'd give it all back," Whittaker said of his jackpot.

[1] An **overdose** is a lethal or toxic amount (of a drug).

Learn

Now that you have finished reading, ask yourself, "What did I learn while reading?" Did you learn what you wanted to? This step is similar to the Review and Recite stages of SQ3R (page 139).

A Write down three or four things you learned from *America's Biggest Lottery Winner* in the Learn column of the chart on page 108.

B Now test how much you learned from the passage by answering the following questions.

1 Why did Jack Whittaker buy a lottery ticket?
   a He played the lottery every day.
   b He knew that he was going to win.
   c He needed money because his business was failing.
   d The prize money was very big.

2 At first, how did Whittaker react to winning $314 million?
   a He kept all the money for himself.
   b He quit his job right away.
   c He was generous with the money.
   d He invested almost all his money.

3 Why did Whittaker say he had no friends?
   a They didn't approve of his new lifestyle.
   b They were all jealous of his money.
   c They only wanted to borrow money from him.
   d They lied to him about illness or bad luck.

4 *He had strayed very far from his original intentions to be humble and sensible.* Where would this sentence best fit?
   a Paragraph 2
   b Paragraph 3
   c Paragraph 4
   d Paragraph 5

5 The phrase *she was "his world"* in line 25–26 means _____.
   a she was very important to him
   b they lived in the same house
   c he was planning to give all his money to her
   d he took her everywhere with him

6 What is the main idea of paragraph 5?
   a Brandi became addicted to illegal drugs.
   b Brandi was a messy and irresponsible person.
   c Brandi's friends were not a good influence on her.
   d Brandi received too much money but not enough guidance.

7 What lesson can be inferred from the story of Jack Whittaker?
   a With enough money, anyone's life is easy.
   b Time is money.
   c Money can't buy happiness.
   d Charity begins at home.

SELF CHECK

Answer the following questions.

1. Have you ever used the KWL method before?

   ☐ Yes   ☐ No   ☐ I'm not sure.

2. Do you think KWL is helpful? Why or why not?

   ☐ Yes   ☐ No   ☐ I'm not sure.

3. Will you use KWL on Review Readings 3 and 4? Why or why not?

   _____

   _____

4. Which of the six reading passages in units 4–6 did you enjoy most? Why?

   _____

   _____

5. Which of the six reading passages in units 4–6 was easiest? Which was the most difficult? Why?

   _____

   _____

6. When you are reading, do you find yourself having to translate? If so, what do you think you can do to minimize this?

   _____

   _____

7. What improvements are you making as a reader? Write down one or two things that you know you can do better today than when you started this course.

   _____

   _____

8. What other improvements do you still want to make as a reader?

   _____

   _____

Review Reading 3: That Unique Japanese Holiday called...Christmas!

Fluency Practice

Time yourself as you read through the passage. Write down your time, then answer the questions on page 115. After answering the questions, correct your responses and write down your score. Record your performance on the Reading Rate Chart on page 240.

THAT UNIQUE JAPANESE HOLIDAY CALLED... CHRISTMAS!

1 Christmas is such a popular holiday that it's no surprise that the Japanese celebrate it as well. To the Western person who visits Japan at the end of the year, many sights and sounds are familiar: the Santas in ads, the big displays and the Christmas music in the stores, the lights on the houses, stockings stuffed with toys, and decorated trees.

2 5 But look a bit closer and you begin to realize that the Japanese interpretation of Christmas is something rather different. For one thing, Christmas is more of a fun start to the holidays rather than the main event. In Japan, the most 10 important holiday of the season is New Year's Day, which comes one week later. New Year is the big traditional holiday when family and friends get together. In fact, Christmas is not officially a holiday at all—most people have 15 to work that day unless it happens to fall on a weekend. As a result, people celebrate on Christmas Eve.

Christmas in Shibuya, Tokyo

3 What do the Japanese do on Christmas Eve? Often they go out for dinner at a fancy restaurant. This custom has become very popular, and most good restaurants are fully

20 booked for that evening. It is the ideal time for couples to go out for a special evening, where they dress up, give each other presents, and enjoy a delicious meal. Christmas has become associated with romance, rather like Valentine's Day in the West.

4 The food is an important part of the Christmas celebrations. Japanese do not usually eat roast turkey or baked ham on
25 Christmas. They are more likely to eat fried or teriyaki chicken, fried potatoes, cheese-stuffed wonton, or even pizza. The favorite dessert is "Christmas cake," which hardly exists in the West. It is a light, not very sweet cake covered with whipped cream and fruit such as strawberries, sometimes with a plastic Santa Claus for decoration
30 on top. Stores everywhere compete to sell their own unique cakes in the days leading up to Christmas.

5 As in the West, gift-giving is a big part of the holiday, but it takes on its own character in Japan. On their big night out, romantic partners may give each other flowers, cute stuffed toys, or rings and other jewelry. Within the family, parents may give presents to 35 their young children, although it's usually not vice versa. The idea here is that the gifts come from Santa Claus, so it only makes sense to give them while the children are still young enough to believe in Santa. It is customary 40 to give presents called *oseibo* to bosses and colleagues, to teachers, or to other people outside the immediate circle of friends and family. These gifts function as a way of showing appreciation to people who have performed 45 some type of service for you.

6 Christians make up only a very small part (less than two percent) of the population of Japan, so people are not very familiar with the religious roots of the holiday. Nevertheless, the Japanese have an amazing ability to import elements from other cultures and integrate them
50 with their own culture. For example, Buddhism, the parliamentary form of government, large corporations, and the current educational system all originally came from abroad. These things are so successful in today's Japan precisely because they are no longer exactly the same as they were. Like Christmas, the Japanese made them uniquely their own.

564 words   Time taken _____

Reading Comprehension

Choose the correct answers for the following questions.

1 What is similar about the Western and Japanese Christmas?
    a Santa Claus is a popular figure.
    b Many people go to church.
    c Christmas cakes are sold everywhere.
    d They don't go to work on Christmas Day.

2 Which is the most important day of the festive season in Japan?
    a Christmas Day
    b Christmas Eve
    c New Year's Day
    d New Year's Eve

3 Which food is NOT popular during the Christmas period in Japan?
    a cake
    b pizza
    c fried chicken
    d roast turkey

4 *But once Christmas is over, they lower the prices dramatically.* This sentence would best fit at the end of
    ____.
    a Paragraph 1
    b Paragraph 2
    c Paragraph 3
    d Paragraph 4

5 Who might a Japanese person give *oseibo* (line 41) to?
    a their young child
    b their best friend
    c their secretary
    d someone they just met

6 What is the main idea of the last paragraph?
    a The Japanese are good at adopting and adapting traditions.
    b The Japanese love foreign cultures.
    c Christmas is not a religious holiday in Japan.
    d Things need to be changed to be successful in Japan.

7 The purpose of this passage is to _____.
    a encourage people to visit Japan for Christmas
    b explain why Christmas is so popular in Japan
    c explore the concept of a Japanese Christmas
    d compare Western and Japanese holidays

Review Reading 4: Natural Mysteries

Time yourself as you read through the passage. Write down your time, then answer the questions on page 118. After answering the questions, correct your responses and write down your score. Record your performance on the Reading Rate Chart on page 240.

NATURAL MYSTERIES

1 Advances in science and technology may have helped us solve many natural mysteries, but there are some that still puzzle scientists. Keep reading for three natural events that science has yet to fully explain.

2
Animal Migration

5 Migration has fascinated humans for centuries. Ancient civilizations puzzled over why large numbers of animals would disappear and reappear at certain times of the year. Many animal species make annual journeys to faraway lands, usually to find food, warmer weather, or places to breed. Distances traveled are often vast. For example, the monarch
10 butterfly flies between 2,000 to 4,500 kilometers (or more) from the U.S. and Canada to forests in central Mexico. There, they hibernate and produce the next generation of butterflies that will make the trip back.

3 How an insect weighing as much as a paper clip can complete such a long journey is one thing. What's more mystifying is how these animals
15 even manage to get to their locations, especially when they've never been taught to do so. The biologist Rupert Sheldrake noted,"Baby green turtles that have hatched on the beaches of Ascension Island, in the middle of the Atlantic, find their way across the ocean to the ancestral[1] feeding grounds off the Brazilian coast. Years later, when the time comes for them to lay their eggs, they then make their way back to Ascension Island, only six 20 miles across and over 1,400 miles away, with no land in between."

Monarch butterflies resting on their journey

4 The main theory is that these migrating animals navigate using the sun, moon, and stars, a magnetic sense, or the sense of smell. But heavenly bodies are not always visible, and the Earth's magnetic field is known to be very unreliable. Also, how would an animal 25 smell its destination from such a distance? It seems many of these creatures just know their way by sheer 30 intuition.

baby green turtles leaving the nest and heading for the ocean

[1] A place that is **ancestral** is a very old place that is visited or lived in before by one's ancestors.

Raining Fish and Frogs

In January 2012, residents of a town in Agusandel Sur, the Philippines, got the shock of their lives
35 when it started raining fish. Many thought the world was coming to an end. But they were just witnesses to a rare phenomenon that has been recorded throughout history and all over the world. People insist there is a simple explanation: strong winds traveling over water may sometimes pick up small items or animals such as fish or frogs before depositing them a few kilometers on.

a 1555 engraving of rain of fish

However, in Depatmento de Yoro of Honduras, it has been raining fish for years and no one has figured out how or why this happens. Every May or June, a heavy rain lasting up to three hours leaves the streets with small fish, many still flapping about. A National Geographic team, which documented the "rainfall" in the 1970s, determined that the fish were all of the same species but were not found anywhere around the area. It is also exceptionally rare to have it occur in the same place twice. Since 1998, the city of Yoro has even organized a festival around this called, appropriately, "The Rain Of Fish Festival"!

Ball Lightning

For centuries, people have reported seeing strange glowing balls of light appear during thunderstorms. Called ball lightning, these tennis- or even beach ball-sized spheres typically glow, spin, hiss, bounce, and float.

ball lightning seen near Nice, France

Graham K. Hubler, a physicist who studies ball lightning, 55 describes an encounter when he was 16 years old. "It's extraordinary—you're so startled that you remember it for the rest of your life," he said. "It drifted along a few feet above the ground, but when it came inside [the pavilion] it dropped down to the ground and skittered[2] along the floor." 60

For years, scientists could not explain the phenomenon. But a pair of Brazilian scientists may have finally solved it by creating ball lightning in a lab in 2007. The pair suggested that when lightning strikes a surface, like the Earth's silica-rich soil, a vapor or gas is formed. 60 This silicon[3] vapor then combines with oxygen in the air and slowly burns. Energy from this chemical reaction causes the resulting ball of electricity to zoom around.

[2] To **skitter** is to move lightly and quickly across a surface.
[3] **Silicon** is a chemical element, while **silica** is a hard substance commonly found in sand or soil.

671 words   **Time taken** _____

Reading Comprehension

1 Which is NOT given as a reason for migration in the passage?
  a to hibernate
  b to reproduce
  c to search for more food sources
  d to spread their species further

2 The word *intuition* in line 32 means _____.
  a knowledge of natural elements
  b something learned from parents
  c natural instinct
  d hard work

3 Which is NOT true about the raining fish phenomenon in Honduras?
  a The fish are all dead when they fall from the sky.
  b The fish are all of the same species.
  c It always happens in the same area.
  d The fish are from outside the immediate area.

4 Which is put forward as a reason for the raining fish phenomenon?
  a It was discovered to be a hoax.
  b It is a scientific experiment.
  c It is due to extreme weather conditions.
  d It is due to flying fish.

5 How did Hubler feel when he saw ball lightning for the first time?
  a terrified
  b fascinated
  c disturbed
  d confused

6 *This recent development may have finally closed the case of this mystery.* Where would this sentence best fit?
  a Paragraph 3
  b Paragraph 6
  c Paragraph 8
  d Paragraph 9

7 What do all three natural phenomena have in common?
  a They are all closed to being solved.
  b They have been observed for centuries.
  c They only happen in certain parts of the world.
  d They are being researched in laboratories.

HEALTHY HABITS QUIZ

Do you . . .	always	sometimes	never
1 have regularly scheduled meals at home?			
2 eat at least one meal a day with your family?			
3 do your grocery shopping when you're full?			
4 adjust portion sizes to your needs?			
5 drink six glasses of water every day?			
6 eat three meals every day?			
7 chew your food slowly?			
8 eat only what you need, instead of finishing everything on your plate?			
9 eat only in certain areas of the house, like the dining room?			
10 use the stairs instead of taking the elevator or escalator?			

Getting Ready

A Complete the survey above by checking (✓) the boxes that apply to you.

B For each "always", give yourself 2 points. For each "sometimes", give yourself 1 point. For each "never", give yourself 0 points. Add up your score, then compare your results below.

What does your total score mean?

18–20   You are on the right track. Keep up with your healthy habits!

11–17   You are doing well, but could work on areas where you answered **sometimes** or **never**.

10 or lower   It's never too late to be healthy! Adopt one or two healthy habits listed above each month and see how you feel.

CHAPTER 1 Successful Dieting

Before You Read
Popular Diets

A Look at these popular dieting plans. How effective do you think each one would be for losing weight? Rank them from 1–5 (1 = most effective).

_____ **The Meat Diet:** By eating mainly meat and avoiding carbohydrates like rice and bread, you will eventually lose weight.

_____ **The Chicken Soup Diet:** You eat breakfast every morning, and then you eat as much chicken soup as you want for the rest of the day.

_____ **The Cabbage Soup Diet:** Some days vegetables are allowed, on other days beef is allowed. If you are hungry, you can have all the cabbage soup you want.

_____ **The Slow Chew Diet:** Chew each mouthful of food 50 times before you swallow it. This will help you enjoy food more and you'll find yourself eating less.

_____ **The One Meal Diet:** You can have only one meal a day. You can eat whatever you want and as much as you want for that meal.

B Discuss your answers with a partner. What other dieting plans do you know?

Reading Skill
Scanning

When we need to find certain information in a text, we move our eyes quickly across the page. When we see the part of the text that might have the information we need, we read only that section. This allows us to save time during tests, when searching for information on the Internet, etc.

A Scan the web forum on the pages 121–122 for the following information. Match each piece of advice with the reason that it helps dieters.

Advice		Reason	
1 _____ eat whole grains	**a**	high in fiber	
2 _____ portion control	**b**	eat what you like in smaller amounts	
3 _____ a vegetarian diet	**c**	keep losing weight over time	
4 _____ exercise	**d**	don't need to change what you eat too much	

B Discuss your answers in **A** with a partner.

C Now read the entire passage carefully. Then answer the questions on page 123.

Motivational Tip: Why is this reading skill important? Why is this reading skill important? You will practice scanning in this chapter, but where can you also use this skill? Think about two other situations in your life where scanning is important. When you realize that a reading skill can be applied beyond the text, your reading will improve.

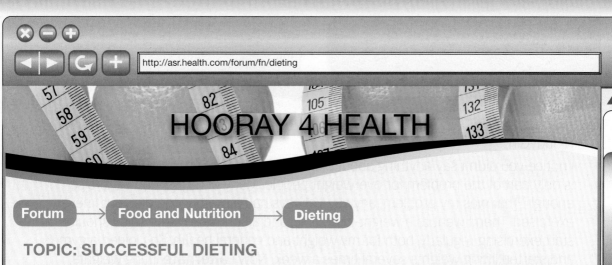

http://asr.health.com/forum/fn/dieting

HOORAY 4 HEALTH

Forum → Food and Nutrition → Dieting

TOPIC: SUCCESSFUL DIETING

Hi everyone,

A question for all you **veteran** dieters out there: What's the best way to lose weight and keep it off? I've tried all kinds of **fad** diets: low fat, low carbohydrate, grapefruit, cabbage soup—you name it, I've tried it! I do lose some weight, but have never been able to keep it off. Plus, eating the same food day after day can be so boring! How do you do it? 5

JudyGirl, Spokane, Washington

Hi JudyGirl,

Fad diets haven't done the trick for me, either. The problem is that you either eat too much of one kind of food and get **fed up with** it, or you don't get enough of 10 the foods that your body needs. So when you stop, you eat too much of the foods that weren't on the diet and the weight comes back. For me the solution has been **portion** control. I have to be aware of serving sizes for each meal and make sure everything is in moderate amounts. For example, for dinner, I'll fix a nice, attractive meal of a piece of meat, some rice, and a salad, and I put everything in front of me. 15 I eat slowly and stop when it's finished—no seconds! And no eating between meals! I eat less but appreciate the food more. This method has really worked for me.

Drew T., Chicago

JudyGirl,

My secret to weight control has been "no white foods." You know, no white bread, 20 pasta, potatoes, or desserts made with white flour and refined sugar. These foods are **loaded with** calories but don't contain much nutrition. You can still eat foods made with whole grains like whole wheat bread, crackers, and oatmeal. These foods are better for you, and they fill you up because they contain a lot of fiber. So think brown foods, not white! 25

QueenMother, London

Hi JudyGirl,

I notice you didn't say anything about exercise. As I'm sure you're aware, food is only part of the problem for overweight people. Many of us just don't exercise enough. That was my problem, anyway. I always had a pretty good diet, but I never exercised. Then I went to a weight-loss clinic, and a counselor there said I should start exercising regularly, both for my weight and general health. So I joined a gym and started lifting weights several times a week. Now I **alternate** lifting weights, swimming, and jogging. Exercise has made a huge difference in my life. I was able to lose ten kilograms without changing my diet very much (though I eat fewer desserts). Also, I've kept off the weight for three years now. You don't need to **go overboard**; getting a few sessions of exercise a week should be enough.

JimGym, **Sydney**

JudyGirl,

Have you thought about becoming a vegetarian? I used to follow a typical American diet—lots of meat, lots of junk food, and I especially loved fast-food hamburgers! I wasn't terribly overweight—maybe five to seven kilograms—but I felt slow and tired all the time. Then a friend told me about the health benefits of a vegetarian diet, and I decided to try it. I didn't lose a lot of weight right away, but I kept losing over time, maybe a couple of pounds a month. What's more important is that I have more energy and feel healthier than ever! It can be a **struggle** to be a vegetarian, though. Sometimes it's difficult to find restaurants with good vegetarian options, and you have to plan your meals more carefully. But, it's been worth it for me—I look better and feel great!

Minjoo, **San Francisco**

Hi everybody,

Many thanks to all of you for your great ideas. Drew T. and QueenMother, I'm definitely going to try portion control and cut down on white foods. And a special appreciation to you, JimGym. You've reminded me that I really need to exercise more. Sorry, Minjoo, while I see how becoming vegetarian could work, I'm not ready to give up meat!
Well, everyone, wish me luck.

JudyGirl

30

35

40

45

50

55

A Choose the correct answer for the following questions.

1 Which is NOT mentioned as a problem with fad diets?
   a You put the weight back on once you stop the diet.
   b You spend a lot of time planning your meals.
   c You get bored eating the same kind of foods.

2 What is the main idea behind portion control?
   a You eat only what you need and nothing more.
   b You arrange your food attractively on your plate.
   c You prepare different kinds of foods.

3 Which is NOT an example of a "white food"?
   a refined sugar   **b** oatmeal   **c** potatoes

4 Why did Minjoo become vegetarian?
   a to be healthier   **b** to lose weight   **c** to save money

5 Whose advice would someone follow if they didn't want to change their diet?
   a QueenMother's   **b** JimGym's   **c** Minjoo's

6 Whose advice did JudyGirl NOT decide to follow?
   a DrewT's   **b** JimGym's   **c** Minjoo's

B Answer the following questions with information from the passage.

1 How has JudyGirl tried to lose weight in the past?
_____
_____

2 According to Drew T., why don't fad diets work?
_____
_____

3 Why does QueenMother think brown foods are better than white foods?
_____
_____

4 According to Minjoo, what are some problems with being vegetarian?
_____
_____

C Discuss the following questions with a partner.

Critical Thinking

1 Which do you think is the most useful piece of advice that JudyGirl received?

2 Would you post a question on the Internet in order to get advice? Why, or why not?

Vocabulary Comprehension
Definitions

A **Choose the best answer. The words in blue are from the passage.**

1 Jim and Sally alternate household chores like washing dishes by
_____.

   a doing them together   **b** taking turns each day

2 Sam struggles with math; he studies hard _____.

   a and gets As   **b** but still fails

3 I didn't expect him to go overboard and buy _____.

   a a small second-hand car   **b** an expensive new sports car

4 Something is a fad when it _____.

   a lasts a long time   **b** is popular for a short while

5 I'm so fed up with this diet; I'm going to _____.

   a quit soon   **b** keep trying

6 Which is loaded with calories?

   a lettuce   **b** cake

7 A veteran usually has _____ experience than other people in
the same field.

   a more   **b** less

8 If someone spends a portion of their money, they spend
_____ of it.

   a all   **b** some

B **Complete the following sentences using the words in blue from A. You
might have to change the form of the word.**

1 I try not to eat pizza too often because it's _____
carbohydrates and fat.

2 To avoid injury, computer users should _____ between using
their right hand and their left hand when using the mouse.

3 Don't _____ and spend all your money the moment you get
your monthly salary.

4 We need to divide up the money so we each get equal _____.

5 I got a tutor because I was _____ with learning Spanish.

6 The hula hoop was a(n) _____ in the 1950s and '60s, but it's
not so popular now.

7 He was an army _____. He has served in the military for 26
years.

8 I'm _____ the rising property prices and cost of living in the
city, so I'm moving to the country.

A Complete the diagram below using the words in the box. Then add other words or phrases you know.

> walk more   fatty foods   lots of carbohydrates
> fiber   in a gym   moderate portions

Vocabulary Skill
Creating Word Webs

One helpful strategy that you can use to memorize new vocabulary is to create a "word web." Word webs can help you remember the meaning of new vocabulary and relate this vocabulary to other words you know.

B Explain your diagram to a partner. Add additional words or phrases to your word web.

C Now try making a word web using words you found in another chapter. See how many branches and words you can add. Share your ideas with a partner.

CHAPTER 2 Barefoot Running

Before You Read
The Right Fit

A Read about the three different types of running style. Which do you use?

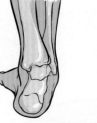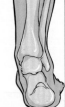

If you're a **pronator**, your ankle rolls inward as you run. This means when your heel hits the ground, the foot moves to the inside as it goes forward.
If you're a **supinator**, your ankle rolls to the outside. The outside of the foot is favored as it moves forward.
If you're a **neutral** runner, your foot and ankle land right in the middle. The foot travels in a straight line as it moves forward.

a pronator

Here's a test to determine your running style:

1 Put a piece of brown paper (like a grocery bag) on the floor. **2** Wet the bottom of your foot and step onto the paper. **3** Check the kind of print you made. A wide print means you are probably a pronator while a narrow print, or one with the middle missing entirely, shows that you are more likely a supinator. You are neutral if it's somewhere in between.

Another test is to check your shoes. If the outside of the shoe is worn down, you're likely to be a supinator. If it's the opposite, you're a pronator. If it's evenly worn down, you're probably neutral!

B Discuss the following questions with a partner.

1 How would your running style affect your shoes? What kind of shoe would suit each style?
2 Do you believe we need shoes to walk or run properly? Why, or why not?

Reading Skill
Predicting

When good readers approach a text, they start asking themselves questions about it right away, even before they start to read. Predicting activates our previous knowledge of the topic and helps us read more effectively.

A Preview the article on the pages 127–128. Look at the title, pictures, and accompanying captions. Then answer the following questions.

1 Barefoot running is (losing / gaining) popularity among athletes.
2 People who run barefoot tend to have (more / fewer) injuries.
3 Some athletes claim going barefoot has made them run (slower / faster).
4 People who run barefoot tend to have (shorter / longer) strides.
5 Running barefoot encourages people to land on the (front / back) of their foot.

B Skim the passage to see whether your predictions in A were correct.

C Now read the entire passage carefully. Then answer the questions on page 129.

Barefoot Running

1 In recent years, the growing trend of barefoot running has started a debate among athletes and doctors about the possible health benefits of running with very light sandals

5 or no shoes at all. Barefoot running has gained popularity among both casual and competitive athletes. Some athletes say that running barefoot has helped them cure or avoid injuries; others claim that running barefoot has improved their running form and race times. Opponents, however, say that there is no scientific or medical proof that

10 barefoot running is safer or better than wearing traditional running shoes.

2

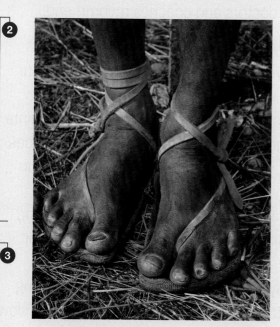

A Tarahumara Indian wears sandals made of used tires.

3 Researchers point out that many of the world's best long-distance running cultures—the Tarahumara Indians of Mexico and the Marathon Monks of Enryaku Temple in Japan, for example—run either barefoot or in thin sandals and don't 15 often suffer leg injuries. These same experts note that certain injuries that are common to shoe-wearing athletes are rare among barefoot running cultures, especially back and knee issues.

Barefoot running supporters believe that going 20 shoeless strengthens foot and calf muscles, improves **balance**, reduces the shock of hitting the ground, and actually makes some runners faster. Researchers have noted that running

25 barefoot encourages runners to land more on the front of the foot—the forefoot or ball of the foot—rather than on the heel, which is what most people do when they run in shoes. This causes a smaller part of the foot to come to a sudden stop when the foot first lands, allowing the natural spring-like motion of the foot and leg to **absorb** any

further shock. By contrast, the "heel striking" style of running by most runners in shoes
30 is said to put stress on leg joints and the back.

4 A 2012 study compared runners wearing shoes and running barefoot. The study
documented a six percent improvement in energy usage when running barefoot.
Because runners without shoes take shorter strides and may have different contact
with the ground, they use less oxygen and feel less tired. According to the study, this
35 level of energy saving is equal to what can be achieved after six weeks of training in
running shoes.

5 Despite this, there is still no **clear-cut** data, and the debate about barefoot running
is alive and well. Doctors and coaches have noted that people who normally run in
shoes have "forgotten" how to run without shoes, and **urge** athletes not to **rush** into
40 barefoot running. **Persistent** pain in the heels, knees, or lower back might be signs
that your running form needs adjusting. For those interested in trying barefoot running,
here are some precautions and practices that doctors and coaches recommend:

- Start slowly. Your feet need time to grow tough skin. Start by walking short
distances without shoes, and increase your distances very slowly to give your
45 body time to **adapt**.
- Listen to your body. In addition to the skin on your feet, your muscles and joints
will need time to get used to walking and running without the support of shoes.
If your feet or muscles **ache**, stop what you're doing and don't increase your
workout until you feel comfortable.
50 - Take care of your muscles. Stretch your legs often and massage your feet and
lower legs to help muscles heal and gain strength. Stretching also helps your
Achilles tendon and feet stay flexible.
- Make sure it feels right. You will naturally be able to feel when you are landing
comfortably on your feet. If you notice too much of a shock when you land, slow
55 down and focus on how your feet are meeting the ground. A gentle landing will
feel almost like bouncing or jumping.

A Read the following sentences. Check (✓) whether they are true (T) or
false (F).

		T	F
1	Barefoot running is a dying sport that is only practiced by a few tribes in Africa.		
2	Many of the world's best running cultures run barefoot or in thin sandals.		
3	There is scientific proof that barefoot running is better for you.		
4	Back and knee injuries are rare among barefoot running cultures.		
5	Running barefoot changes the way that the foot strikes the ground.		
6	Studies have found that it takes more energy to run barefoot.		
7	The heel strike is currently the most common running style.		
8	Feeling pain when running barefoot indicates that your running form needs adjustment.		

B Read the following subheadings. Match them to the correct sections by
writing the paragraph numbers from 1–5.

_____   Energy-efficient Running
_____   Taking Your First Steps
_____   The Barefoot Debate
_____   Physical Benefits?
_____   Barefoot Cultures

C Discuss the following questions with a partner.

Critical Thinking

1   Would you want to run barefoot? Why, or why not?
2   Why do you think there is a movement towards a more "natural" lifestyle,
    such as barefoot running and eating organic foods?

Vocabulary Comprehension

Odd Word Out

A (Circle) the word or phrase that does not belong in each group. The words in blue are from the passage.

1	transfer	shift	move	absorb
2	balance	combination	mixture	blend
3	thankful	persistent	grateful	appreciative
4	persuade	urge	resist	promote
5	joy	pain	soreness	ache
6	rush	hurry	relax	quicken
7	adapt	avoid	escape	run
8	definite	clear-cut	obvious	confusing

B Complete the following sentences with the words in blue from **A**. You might have to change the form of the word.

1 Thanks to his email records, John has _____ evidence of how his employers mistreated him.

2 Sports towels are made out of a special fabric that _____ water very easily.

3 An intelligent person usually _____ quickly to various challenges.

4 I missed a step, lost my _____, and fell over.

5 Sorry, I need to _____ off. I have to meet my friend in ten minutes!

6 The best salespeople are _____ and won't take no for an answer.

7 I know you've made your decision, but I strongly _____ you to reconsider.

8 My back is really _____ from helping my friend pack and move house yesterday.

Motivational Tip: Success or failure? Effort or ability? When you succeed, is it because of your effort or your ability? Success can be a combination of both of these things, but effort is perhaps more important. When you succeed, remember that it is because of the time you spent working toward your goal. When you fail, remember it is not because you are bad at it, but because you need to devote more time and energy to achieving success.

A Look at the following chart featuring words with the prefix *fore*. Check (✓) whether they are nouns (N) and/or verbs (V). Then, with a partner, write a short definition for each word.

Vocabulary Skill
The Prefix *fore-*

	Word	V	N	Definition
1	forecast			
2	forehead			
3	foresee			
4	forefathers			
5	forearm			
6	forefront			
7	forewarn			
8	foreword			
9	foreboding			
10	foreground			

In this chapter you read the word *forefoot*. The prefix *fore* is an old English word that means *before* (in space, time, condition, etc.). It can also refer to something that's superior, or physically in front.

B Complete the following sentences with the correct form of the words from **A**. You might have to change the form of the word.

1 My _____ came from England and Ireland in the 18th century.
2 You didn't focus the camera properly. All the subjects in the _____ are blurred.
3 Companies have to be flexible and innovative in order to stay at the _____ of their industry.
4 I am getting my university professor to write a _____ for my new book.
5 I think I'm getting a fever; my _____ feels really warm.
6 You should bring an umbrella to work. It's been _____ to rain today.
7 The city council _____ residents that the construction work for the new town hall might cause traffic jams due to road closures.
8 When you grip onto something, you are working the muscles of your _____ .
9 Before I heard the bad news, I already had a sense of _____ that something would go wrong.
10 I wish I had _____ that housing prices would fall. I wouldn't have bought an apartment so soon!

Real Life Skill

Understanding Common Health Terms

In this unit, you encountered a number of health and fitness terms. Knowing some of these terms can help you better understand health and fitness literature. A few of them also have abbreviations which may be more commonly used.

A Look at the following health and fitness terms. With a partner, discuss what you think they mean.

1 Body Mass Index (BMI)
2 heart rate
3 Resting Metabolic Rate (RMR)
4 body composition
5 resistance training
6 blood pressure
7 warm-up/cool-down
8 Glycemic Index (GI)
9 ultraviolet (UV)

B Circle the correct word(s) to complete the following sentences.

1 Your BMI is an estimate of your body fat based on your (age / weight and height).
2 Your heart rate is usually measured as the number of times your heart beats per (second / minute).
3 Your RMR is a measure of the amount of (energy you use / breaths you take) while you are at rest.
4 Your body composition depends on the amount of (fat, bone, and blood / muscle in your body).
5 (Weight lifting / Yoga) is an example of resistance training.
6 In general, the (lower / higher) your blood pressure, the more at risk you are at having heart disease.
7 Athletes do warm-up exercises (before / after) taking part in a race.
8 Your GI is a measure of how quickly your blood sugar levels (rise / fall) after eating a particular type of food.
9 Too much exposure to UV radiation can cause (skin cancer / heart disease).

C Now do an Internet search for the terms in **A** and check your answers for **B**.

What do you think?

1 Are people in your country generally healthy? What is their diet like? What do they do for exercise?
2 Do you think the idea of health and fitness is different from culture to culture? Why, or why not?
3 If you worked for the government, how would you encourage people to lead a healthy lifestyle?

Space and Flight

Getting Ready

Discuss the following questions with a partner.

1 Name as many of the vehicles above as you can.
2 In what order were these vehicles invented? Number them from 1–5 (1 = oldest invention).
3 Which countries have space programs? What are their accomplishments?

CHAPTER 1 Human Adaptation to Space

Before You Read
Life in Space

A Answer the following questions.

1 What do you know about the job of an astronaut? What kind of work does an astronaut do in space?

2 Do you think an astronaut's job is dangerous? Can you remember any accidents involving spaceflight?

3 How do you think space travel affects an astronaut's body?

B Discuss your answers with a partner.

Reading Skill
Identifying Main and Supporting Ideas

Most paragraphs have a main idea, or topic, that tells us what that paragraph is about. Often, you will find the main idea is in the first or second sentence of a paragraph. Supporting ideas usually follow the main idea. Sentences containing supporting ideas explain or give us more information about the main idea.

A Read the following sentences from the passage on the pages 135–136. Write M next to the statement that is the main idea of the paragraph. Write S next to the supporting idea.

Paragraph 2

1 _____ Many astronauts suffer physical problems on these missions, even if they are in space for just a few months.

2 _____ More than two-thirds of all astronauts suffer from motion sickness while traveling in space.

Paragraph 3

3 _____ Being in a weightless environment means that astronauts tend not to use the muscles they rely upon on Earth, so their muscles gradually atrophy.

4 _____ For the duration of their mission, astronauts experience conditions that affect their health.

Paragraph 4

5 _____ The irregular sleep, long working hours, and the lack of night and day can affect a person's emotions and stress level.

6 _____ In addition to physical difficulties, astronauts who travel for long periods may also suffer from psychological stress.

B Discuss your answers in A with a partner. Then skim the paragraphs to check if your answers are correct.

C Now read the entire passage carefully. Then answer the questions on page 137.

Human Adaptation to Space

1 In April 1961, Russian cosmonaut Yuri Gagarin made history when he became the first man to travel in space. On July 20, 1969, American astronaut Neil Armstrong became the first man to walk on the
5 Moon. Now that humans have been to the Moon and robots have been sent to Mars, some people believe the next step is for humans to visit Mars. There's no doubt that the first person to walk on Mars will become as famous as Gagarin or Armstrong, and
10 many astronauts would love the opportunity. But what is space travel really like for the men and women who go on these **missions**?

cover of the December 1969 issue of
National Geographic Magazine

2

In zero gravity, astronauts can support each other with one finger.

Many astronauts suffer physical problems on these missions, even if they are in space for just a few months. Some of these problems are short-lived; others may be   15
long-lasting. More than two-thirds of all astronauts suffer from motion sickness while traveling in space. In an environment without gravity, the body cannot tell up from down. The body's internal balance system sends confusing signals to the brain, which can result in nausea[1] lasting as   20
long as a few days. The amount of blood and other fluids in the body also ends up being **distributed** differently after an extended period of time in this environment. More fluid than normal ends up in the face, neck, and chest, resulting in a puffy face, bulging neck veins, and a slightly enlarged heart.   25

3 For the **duration** of their mission, astronauts experience conditions that affect their health. For example, their bones get weaker and they may lose muscle. Being in a

[1] **Nausea** is a feeling of sickness that may cause one to vomit.

weightless environment means that astronauts tend not to use the muscles they rely upon on Earth, so their muscles gradually atrophy.[2] This, combined with the shift of
30 fluid to the upper body and the resulting loss of essential minerals (such as calcium), causes bones to weaken. As a result, many astronauts are unable to walk properly for a few days upon their return to Earth. In addition, they are **exposed** to radiation[3] from the sun, which is more **intense** without the Earth's atmosphere to protect them. This puts them at a higher risk of cancer.

4 35 In addition to physical difficulties, astronauts who travel for long periods may also suffer from psychological stress. Space travel requires astronauts to be very focused, balanced people. The irregular sleep, long working hours, and the lack of night and day can affect a person's emotions and stress level. Being able to control one's emotions is an important characteristic for an astronaut.

5 40 A major factor that affects astronauts' mental well-being is time. To date, astronauts have only spent a few months in space at a time, but longer **expeditions** would require astronauts to spend significantly more time inside a spaceship. For example, a round-trip expedition to Mars could take about three years. Being **confined** in a small space for such a long period of time is not healthy. Research has shown that travelers
45 on such long journeys—such as sailors or explorers in the Arctic—have an above-average chance of suffering from depression.

6 Astronauts—especially those who
50 achieved significant "firsts" such as Gagarin and Armstrong—are often seen as exciting adventurers. This may be accurate, but it's also worth remembering their dedication and the **sacrifices** they
55 make to explore our universe.

Even in the International Space Station, conditions are very cramped.

[2] To **atrophy** is to become weak, or to lose size and strength.
[3] **Radiation** is heat or light from something such as the sun, a microwave, or X-rays that can be harmful to humans.

A **Choose the correct answers for the following questions.**

1 According to the passage, what is the status of the Mars missions?
   a Mars is still unexplored.
   b Robots have been sent to Mars.
   c People have landed on Mars.
2 What happens to the amount of fluids in an astronaut's body when in space?
   a It generally increases in all parts of the body.
   b It decreases in the upper parts of the body.
   c It increases in some parts and decreases in others.
3 Which condition only affects astronauts' health in the short term?
   a the lack of gravity
   b exposure to the sun's radiation
   c being confined for a long time
4 What do astronauts, sailors, and Arctic explorers NOT have in common?
   a They work in environments without gravity.
   b They have higher rates of depression.
   c They usually go on long journeys.
5 What could be another title for this reading passage?
   a The First Man on Mars
   b The Problems with Space Travel
   c What Makes a Good Astronaut?

B **Read the following sentences. Check (✓) whether they are true (T) or false (F).**

		T	F
1	Russia was the first country to send people to the moon.		
2	Motion sickness is caused by the redistribution of fluids in the body.		
3	The body's balance system needs gravity to work properly.		
4	Astronauts lose muscle because they are exposed to radiation.		
5	An astronaut has to be strong mentally and physically.		
6	The longest time an astronaut has been in space so far is three years.		

Critical Thinking

C **Discuss the following questions with a partner.**

1 Why do you think people still want to be astronauts?
2 Can you think of other occupations which can be harmful to a person's physical or mental health?

Vocabulary Comprehension
Vocabulary in Context

A **Choose the best answer. The words in blue are from the passage.**

1 If you make a sacrifice, you _____.
    a receive something   **b** give something up

2 In which setting might you feel confined?
    a in a small room with no windows   **b** in a park

3 Someone who is on a mission usually _____ a sense of purpose.
    a has   **b** does not have

4 You _____ the temperature if you want intense heat.
    a turn up   **b** turn down

5 You should distribute the money so that _____.
    a everyone gets some   **b** it's in a safe place

6 The duration of the musical was _____.
    a very entertaining   **b** two hours

7 Your legs will be exposed when you wear _____.
    a shorts   **b** trousers

8 Which is an example of an expedition?
    a a two-week research trip in the mountains
    b a trip to the supermarket

B **Answer the following questions, then discuss your answers with a partner. The words in blue are from the passage.**

1 Do you believe wild animals should be confined, for example, in zoos?
2 What is the biggest sacrifice you've ever made for someone?
3 What are some things you would pack on a jungle expedition?
4 Can you think of a situation where you were under intense pressure?
5 What kinds of jobs require people to go on missions?
6 Is there an even distribution of wealth in your country?
7 How can you protect your skin from being exposed to the sun?
8 What is the duration of a typical movie?

Motivational Tip: Strengthen your personal relationships. Your friends can help you achieve your reading goals. Sharing your goals with friends can also strengthen your personal relationships. As you progress through this unit, share with a friend what you've learned and what you hope to learn about space and flight that will help you become a better user of English.

A Complete the following sentences using the words with prefixes *de-* and *dis-* in the box. You might have to change the form of the word.

> deduct   detach   discharge   depart   disqualify

1 At what time is our plane scheduled to _____?
2 The athlete was _____ after it was discovered he'd taken drugs to win the competition.
3 When you hand in your application, _____ and return the lower part of the document, and keep the upper part for your records.
4 After serving in the military for two years, Jin Ho received an honorable _____ from the army.
5 If you turn your test paper in late, Professor Yeo will _____ ten points from your score.

B Now use either *de-* or *dis-* to complete the sentences below. You may use a dictionary to help you.

1 The plane is about to make its _____scent into Tokyo. We should be arriving in about 20 minutes.
2 When Michiko lit a cigarette in the restaurant, the other customers gave her _____approving looks.
3 Unfortunately, her last project failed and may _____tract from her other achievements.
4 When we get off the plane we have to _____embark through the door on the left.
5 At the end of the concert the crowd began to _____perse. Within 20 minutes almost everyone had left the building.

C Can you think of an antonym (word with the opposite meaning) for each of the words in this exercise? Share your ideas with a partner.

Vocabulary Skill
The Prefixes *dis-* and *de-*

In this chapter you learned that astronauts can become depressed. To depress means to *lessen* or to *cause to sink*; you also read the noun *distribution*, meaning the *division or separation of something*. The prefix *de-* means *reduce*, *remove*, or *not*. Dis- means *apart*, as well as *not*. These are two very common prefixes that come before nouns, verbs, adjectives, and adverbs to form many words in English.

CHAPTER 2 Pioneers of Flight

Before You Read
The History of Aviation

A Read about three famous aviation (flight) pioneers.

Amelia Earhart was the first woman to fly alone across the Atlantic Ocean.

The Wright brothers, Orville and Wilbur, were two American inventors who built the world's first successful airplane.

B Discuss the following questions with a partner.

1 What were some challenges that these people might have faced?
2 Can you think of other famous figures in aviation history?

Reading Skill
Making Inferences

Information in a reading passage is not always stated directly. Sometimes a reader has to infer, or make guesses, about events or a writer's opinion or meaning, from the information that is available in the reading.

A Read the following sentences from the passage on the pages 141–142. What can you infer from them? (Circle) the correct answer.

1 *What followed was a huge explosion: Wan Hu and his primitive spaceship had disappeared completely.* (lines 15–17)
   Wan Hu most likely (had a successful flight into space / was blown up by the explosion).

2 *Like other pioneers in the field of transportation, Hughes was simply ahead of his time.* (lines 37–38)
   The Spruce Goose was considered a success (at the time of completion / only many years later).

3 *He wanted to build machines with flapping wings which would be controlled and steered by human pilots, but his dreams remained just that—dreams.* (lines 43–46)
   Leonardo da Vinci (managed / did not manage) to build his flying machines.

B Discuss your answers in **A** with a partner.

C Now read the entire passage carefully. Then answer the questions on page 143.

Pioneers of Flight

Throughout the ages, inventors have been labeled dreamers for daring to imagine possibilities beyond what already exists. Of course, many have proven their critics wrong and brought their ideas to life, thus changing the world and the way we live. Here are three inventors who refused to give up on the "impossible" idea of human
5 flight.

The Legend of Wan Hu

On October 15, 2003, China launched its first proper spaceship. Astronaut Yang Liwei was the first Chinese national sent into space, thus fulfilling a dream that had its roots in a much earlier time. Legend has it that in A.D. 1500 a man named Wan Hu prepared
10 his own mission into space. At that time, the Chinese invention of gunpowder was widely used in rockets for military purposes as well as in fireworks. Wan Hu **devised** a risky plan to use the power of such rockets to take him to the stars.

The story goes that Wan Hu built the first spaceship: a chair with powerful gunpowder rockets and two kites attached to it. On the day of the launch, each of the 47 rockets
15 was lit, by 47 servants carrying torches. The servants then moved back and waited. What followed was a huge explosion: Wan Hu and his **primitive** spaceship had disappeared completely. Although the story may seem a little **far-fetched**, Wan Hu's crazy plan involving rocket power actually contained the basic **principles** of spaceflight.

Howard Hughes's Spruce Goose

20 On November 2, 1947, a crowd of people at San Pedro Harbor in Los Angeles **witnessed** an important moment in flight history. An enormous flying boat, nicknamed the Spruce Goose, sped across the bay and rose 70 feet (21 meters) above
25 the water. After just under a minute, it landed perfectly one mile (1.6 kilometers) down the bay. It was the first and last time the boat ever flew.

the Spruce Goose prepares to take off

The concept for construction of the Spruce Goose came from the need for more effective ways of transporting people and materials in World War II. The idea came
30 from a man called Henry Kaiser, but it was Howard Hughes, the legendary multi-millionaire, who actually developed the flying boat. It was the biggest airplane ever built—it still holds the record for the greatest wingspan[1]—and it was made entirely of wood.

In the end, though, the project failed for various reasons: it was too expensive to operate, working with wood was slow and difficult, and Hughes's desire for perfection
35 caused the project to finish **behind schedule**. By the time the Spruce Goose was completed, the war was long over. However, many of its design features have been incorporated into modern planes. Like other pioneers in the field of transportation, Hughes was simply ahead of his time.

a flying machine based on one of Leonardo da Vinci's designs

The Futuristic Ideas of Leonardo da Vinci

Centuries before the Spruce Goose, another inventor was
40 planning a different kind of flying machine. Leonardo da Vinci, perhaps the most famous artist of the Renaissance[2] period, was inspired by the science of how birds fly. He wanted to build machines with flapping wings which would be controlled and **steered** by human pilots, but his dreams remained just that—
45 dreams. It took almost 500 years for Leonardo's ideas to be tested. In June 2000, a professional parachutist named Adrian Nicholas jumped out of a hot-air balloon over the South African countryside. He used a parachute made of wood and canvas[3] based on one of Leonardo's designs. Nicholas landed safely, and
50 Leonardo's dream became reality.

These three individuals—Wan Hu, Howard Hughes, and Leonardo da Vinci—came from places and cultures that are about as different as we can imagine. What they shared was a fascination with flying, a spirit of **innovation**, and the courage to make their dreams come true.
55

---

[1] The **wingspan** is the distance from the tip of one wing to the tip of the other.
[2] The **Renaissance** period was a rich cultural and artistic period ranging from the 14th to the 17th century.
[3] **Canvas** is a tough plain-woven fabric used for making sails and tents, etc.

A Read the following sentences. Check (✓) if each sentence is true for Wan Hu (W), Howard Hughes (H), and/or Leonardo da Vinci (L).

		W	H	L
1	He was trying to do something that was considered impossible.			
2	His ideas were adopted by other people later on.			
3	The machine was built and managed to fly successfully.			
4	The story of his invention may not be real.			
5	This inventor was also an artist.			

B Answer the following questions with information from the passage.

1 Why does the writer mention China's space flight in 2003?

_____

_____

2 How did Wan Hu power his spaceship?

_____

_____

3 Why was the Spruce Goose flight considered an "important moment in flight history"?

_____

_____

4 Why did the Spruce Goose fail?

_____

_____

5 How were Leonardo da Vinci's designs finally tested?

_____

_____

C Discuss the following questions with a partner.

Critical Thinking

1 Which of these three pioneers do you think was the most interesting, and why?

2 Can you think of other feats that people said could never be achieved but eventually were?

Motivational Tip: A valuable skill. Thinking critically after completing a reading comprehension task is an important step toward becoming a more independent learner. How can this critical thinking activity help you understand the passage and topic better? How can it help you beyond the classroom?

Vocabulary Comprehension

Odd Word Out

A (Circle) the word or phrase that does not belong in each group. The words in blue are from the passage.

1	create	innovate	invent	copy
2	steer	walk	direct	guide
3	late	behind schedule	exact	delayed
4	hard to believe	external	unlikely	far-fetched
5	imagine	see	watch	witness
6	principles	rules	laws	languages
7	futuristic	advanced	primitive	modern
8	devise	transfer	design	plan

B Complete the sentences using the words in blue from **A**. You might have to change the form of the word.

1 Scientists found _____ tools such as stone hammers at the ancient burial site.

2 Companies must be _____ and take risks in order to survive in this competitive world.

3 I think the idea that human life expectancy will increase to 200 years is _____ .

4 We have yet to _____ a machine that is truly capable of independent thought.

5 The captain accidentally _____ the ship too close to shore and hit some rocks.

6 My grandfather _____ many horrible things during the war.

7 Trina missed her connecting flight because her first plane was so far _____ .

8 Scientists can make predictions about outer space by following basic scientific _____ .

A Look at these two idioms related to time. Complete the sentences with the correct idiom. Using the sentences to help you, write a simple definition for *ahead of time*.

> *ahead of one's time*: too modern or forward thinking for the time period one lives in
> *ahead of time*: _____

    a I thought Marcus was coming at 8:00, but he arrived _____ at 7:30.

    b Amelia Earhart was one of the first female aviators. She was truly _____ .

B Do the same for the idiom pairs below. Discuss your answers with a partner.

1 *at a time*: in a certain specific number
   for some time: _____

    a Okay everyone; please enter the theater two _____ .
    b Ms. Yang lived in Taiwan _____ , but she doesn't anymore.

2 *in no time*: _____
   in time: after a certain amount of time has passed, usually a while

    a We're almost at the beach; it's only about another kilometer. We'll be there _____ .

    b Don't worry! You'll learn to write well in Chinese _____ , but it'll take a while.

3 *all the time*: happening continuously, regularly
   of all time: _____

    a I think that Thomas Edison is one of the greatest inventors _____ .

    b My computer keeps crashing _____ so I can't make any progress with this report.

4 *for a time*: for a short period of time
   for the time being: _____

    a You can sit at Hannah's desk _____ , but when she comes back you'll have to move.

    b Junko and Koji dated _____ , but I don't think they are still together.

Vocabulary Skill
Idioms with *time*: Inferring Meaning from Context

> In this chapter, you read the idiom *ahead of one's time*. An idiom is a fixed group of words that has a special meaning. There are many idioms that are formed using the word *time*. Sometimes it's possible to know what the idiom means by looking at the individual words, but it can also be helpful to look at the surrounding words in order to understand its meaning.

Real Life Skill

Dictionary Usage: Identifying Parts of Speech

When you learn new words in English, it is also helpful to learn their parts of speech so that you understand how to use them in sentences. You can use your dictionary to learn a word's part of speech, as well as related word forms (e.g. stress, stressed, stressful).

A Below are some of the parts of speech that appear in dictionaries. Work with a partner to complete the chart.

Part of Speech	Description	Example
noun (*n.*)	person, place, or thing	Tom has a lot of *stress* in his life.
verb (*v.*)		Jessica *studies* Spanish.
adjective (*adj.*)		Fumiko had a *stressful* day. She felt *stressed*.
adverb (*adv.*)		He read the paper *carefully*.
phrasal verb (*phr. v.*)		Hiromi *handed in* her paper.
conjunction (*conj.*)	joins two or more words, sentences, or ideas	Where are my hat *and* coat?
preposition (*prep.*)	describes time and location; makes a comparison between things	The cup is *on* the table. Your name is *after* mine on the list.

B Read the following sentences. For each *italicized* word or phrase, write the correct part of speech from **A**. You may use a dictionary to help you.

1 I can't *keep up with* my work this week. _____
2 Mark has a *spontaneous* sense of humor. _____
3 There hasn't been a war here for six *decades*. _____
4 Hotel prices are cheaper *during* the off-season. _____
5 Maria is searching *frantically* for her lost keys. _____
6 The couple *adopted* a child with no parents. _____
7 One drop of water in the desert is *insignificant*. _____
8 My friends *made fun of* my terrible haircut. _____
9 I resemble my mother, *but* I don't look like my father at all. _____
10 Meteorologists *are speculating* about where the storm will hit. _____

What do you think?

1 Why do you think humans are so fascinated with the idea of flight?
2 In what ways do you think air travel will change in the future?
3 Are there any pioneers in other fields that you admire? Give your reasons.

The Changing Family

Discuss the following questions with a partner.

1 Match these terms with the photos above. What does each term mean?
   a extended family   **b** childfree couple   **c** nuclear family   **d** single-parent family
2 Is it common in your country for several generations of a family to live together in the same home? Why, or why not?
3 Are people in your country having more or fewer children these days? Why?

UNIT 9   **CHAPTER 1** Is an Only Child a Lonely Child?

Before You Read
Family Options

A Read the following sentences. Check (✓) whether you agree (A) or disagree (D).

		A	D
1	Children should grow up close to their grandparents.		
2	It is too expensive to raise children nowadays.		
3	A married couple should have children.		
4	It is better to grow up with many brothers and sisters.		
5	A single parent family is not good for the child.		
6	Mothers are better at caring for children than fathers.		
7	It is possible for a family to be too big.		
8	The pressures of modern life are making families smaller.		

B Discuss your answers with a partner.

Reading Skill
Recognizing Facts and Opinions

A fact is something that can be proven true. An opinion is what the writer believes to be true. This is usually signaled by *in my opinion, believe, think, might, may, probably, should,* etc. Knowing the difference between facts and opinions is important when doing any kind of research.

A Scan the passage on the pages 149–150 for the following information. Check (✓) whether each statement is a fact (F) or an opinion (O).

		F	O
1	An only child does not have brothers or sisters to play with.		
2	An only child gets lonely when the parents are working.		
3	An only child doesn't learn to negotiate with others.		
4	The number of one-child families is increasing in Asia.		
5	There are fewer family arguments with just one child.		
6	What is appropriate for one family may not be appropriate for another.		

B <u>Underline</u> the words in the passage that helped you decide your answer. Discuss your answers with a partner.

C Read the entire passage carefully. Then answer the questions on page 151.

Modern Family Magazine
Is An Only Child a Lonely Child?

This month in *Modern Family*, child psychologist Dr. Ethan Stephens answers a question from Andrea Gonzales, who writes:

Dear Dr. Stephens,

5   My husband and I are facing a **dilemma**, namely, the issue of whether to have a second child. We already have one healthy, happy five-year-old son. Both of us have demanding jobs and limited time and financial resources, but we also want to make sure that our only
10   child does not become a lonely child. What are the pros and cons of having a second child?

Dear Andrea,

This is one of the most difficult issues that parents nowadays face. As you point out, a concern that is often heard with regard to only children is whether one child
15   necessarily means a lonely child. Many parents feel a **stigma** associated with their decision to have only one child, fearing they are seen as thinking only about themselves as opposed to about their child's well-being. There are no other children in the family for the child to associate with, which may lead to the child feeling lonely, especially if both parents are working.

20   Another common argument against having just one child is that an only child may be more spoiled than one with **siblings**. Many people believe that a single child will not have learned to **negotiate** with others or respect the give-and-take involved in many relationships. Some think this may leave the child less capable of interacting well with people his or her own age than one who has been raised with siblings.

25   Your son is not alone in being an only child. There's an increasing trend for choosing to have only one child for the very same reasons you listed. In South Korea, for example,

the percentage of families with only one child is higher than ever. This follows a general trend in Asia where in many countries—including Japan, China, Singapore, and Thailand—couples are having on average fewer than two children.

Advocates of single-child families argue that there 30 are advantages for the child as well as the parents. With just one child, they suggest, there is less potential for family arguments arising from sibling jealousy or parents favoring one child over the other(s). Moreover, with only one child, the parents 35 can afford to give more quality time and attention. This often leads to increased **self-esteem**, which, combined with increased independence, can lead to the child being more confident. There are a number of ways that parents can help to ensure that their only child doesn't get lonely. Here 40 are some suggestions for parenting an only child:

- Let them be social. Children need friends their age and playing in a group encourages skills like sharing, teamwork, and patience. Find ways for your child to socialize, such as play groups, sports, or summer camp.
- 45 • Welcome challenges. Only children learn to do many things for themselves, though they will need your help for some things. Encourage your child to challenge himself by solving problems independently.
- Alone time is okay, too. As much as you want to help your child interact well with others, don't worry too much about a child who is **content** to keep to himself. Time 50 spent alone contributes to personality development and decision-making skills.

Unfortunately, Andrea, there is no simple answer to the question of whether or not to have a second child. The **circumstances** affecting each set of parents are unique; I always believe what is appropriate for one family may not be for another. The important thing, in the end, is to make a decision that both you and your husband feel 55 confident about.

A **Choose the correct answer for the following questions.**

1 What is Ethan Stephens' main job?
   a He studies the way children behave and think.
   b He treats sick children at the hospital.
   c He writes for *Modern Family* magazine.

2 Parents with an only child feel they are seen as _____.
   a selfish for not giving their child a sibling
   b selfish for spending too much time at work
   c sad for being unable to have another child

3 Why does Dr. Stephens talk about family trends in Asia?
   a to convince Andrea that she should stick with just one child
   b to give examples of countries that Andrea and her husband can move to
   c to show that Andrea and her husband are not alone in making this choice

4 Spending time alone can have a positive effect on a child's _____.
   a negotiation skills   b personality   c ability to share

5 Which is NOT mentioned as an advantage of being an only child?
   a They are usually more independent.
   b They are usually more intelligent.
   c They are in a less stressful family environment.

B **Read the following sentences. Check (✓) whether they are true (T) or false (F).**

		T	F
1	Andrea is worried because her son is not happy.		
2	Children with siblings are usually more willing to share things.		
3	An only child should spend time with other children around the same age.		
4	Parents should be worried if a child likes to be alone.		
5	Dr. Stephens suggests that Andrea not have another child.		

C **Discuss the following questions with a partner.**

Critical Thinking

1 If you were Andrea, what would you choose to do? Why?
2 What problems may some of the countries Dr. Stephens discusses face if couples continue to only have one child? What can governments do to adjust to this trend?

Vocabulary Comprehension
Odd Word Out

A (Circle) the word or phrase that does not belong in each group. The words in blue are from the reading.

1	dilemma	solution	problem	difficulty
2	stigma	shame	respect	disgrace
3	believer	supporter	advocate	enemy
4	discuss	insist	cooperate	negotiate
5	satisfied	content	pleased	jealous
6	circumstances	trip	travel	tour
7	self-confidence	self-worth	self-esteem	selfishness
8	brother	sister	veteran	sibling

B Complete the letter below using the words in blue from **A**. You might have to change the form of the word.

Dear Dr. Stephens,

I read with interest your reply to Andrea Gonzales about whether or not she and her husband should have another child. I am facing a similar **(1)** _____ related to having children: my fiancé wants us to start a family after we are married, but I don't.

I realize that every couple encounters different **(2)** _____ in their marriage, but this is one thing I am not willing to **(3)** _____. I don't want to be a mother. My main reason for not wanting to be a parent is that I am a 28-year-old woman who has a demanding job which I love. I am **(4)** _____ with my decision to focus on my career rather than have children. To add the responsibilities of children to my already busy life would be unfair to myself and to the children.

Unfortunately, my fiancé does not feel the same way (he comes from a large family and has many **(5)** _____), nor, to my surprise, do many of my female friends. You can't imagine the **(6)** _____ attached to a woman who says she doesn't want children.

Honestly, some people are such firm **(7)** _____ of having children, they look at me like I'm a monster! I must admit my **(8)** _____ has suffered terribly in the past few months, and I sometimes wonder if I am making the right decision. If I choose not to have children, I know, too, that my fiancé will probably not want to get married. What should I do?

Mariah
Miami, Florida

A Look at how compound nouns are formed. What parts of speech are joined together to form each?

Vocabulary Skill
Compound Nouns

In this chapter, you learned the compound nouns *give-and-take* and *self-esteem*. Compound nouns are two or more words that work together to talk about one person, place, or thing.

1 Some compound nouns join two words together to form one word.

> *birthrate*   *software*   *takeout*

2 Some compound nouns are two words that work together to refer to one thing.

> *family planning*   *maternity leave*   *family tree*

3 Some compound nouns are formed by joining two or more words together with hyphens.

> *self-esteem*   *give-and-take*   *mother-in-law*

B Match the words in the box with the words below to form compound nouns. Is each compound written as one word or two words, or is it hyphenated? You may use a dictionary to help you.

> friend   sitter   style   mother
> control   license   in-law   wife

a father   _____
b boy   _____
c self   _____
d baby   _____
e driver's   _____
f house   _____
g grand   _____
h life   _____

C Match each compound noun from **B** with the correct definition below.

1 _____ a person who takes care of children while the parents are out
2 _____ a woman who stays home and takes care of the house and children
3 _____ a male companion
4 _____ the male parent of one's spouse
5 _____ your father's or mother's mother
6 _____ someone's chosen way of living
7 _____ legal permission to drive a car
8 _____ the ability to remain calm and not show one's feelings; will-power

Motivational Tip: Reading in English is important. Being able to read well in English will help you to achieve success inside and outside of the classroom. As you make progress in this chapter, it will help you as you set and reach your goals outside of the classroom.

CHAPTER 2 Changing Roles: The Rise of Stay-at-Home Dads

Before You Read
Family Responsibilities

A Who would you normally associate the following family responsibilities with? Check (✓) whether you think it should be the man or woman.

	man	woman
making money		
cleaning the house		
doing the laundry		
paying the bills		
disciplining children		
cooking meals		
caring for children		
fixing things		
driving to places		
entertaining guests		

B Discuss your answers with a partner.

Reading Skill
Previewing

Previewing is something good readers do when they first encounter new reading material. They ask themselves questions like these: *What is this about? What kind of text is this? What do I already know about it?* Previewing can involve skimming, scanning, and predicting to help us get acquainted with the reading passage.

A Preview the passage on the pages 155–156. Look at the title and pictures, scan for any interesting information, and skim the first and last paragraphs.

B Now discuss the following questions with a partner.

1 What do you think the passage is about?
2 Where could you find this kind of article?
3 What do you already know about this subject?
4 What interesting points did you notice?
5 Do you think you'll enjoy reading about this topic?

C Now read the entire passage carefully. Then answer the questions on page 157.

Changing Roles: The Rise of Stay-at-Home Dads

As little as 50 years ago, few people in the U.S. questioned the gender roles that had been in place for centuries. Many people assumed that a woman's place was in the home, and that a man's main responsibility to his family was to put food on the table. In the 1970s and 80s, however, greater numbers of working women meant that men
5   were no longer the **sole** breadwinners.[1] A father's involvement with his family also became more important. Even so, back then, almost no husbands were "stay-at-home dads." Today, with more career opportunities than ever available to women, the stay-at-home dad trend is on the rise.

A family with a full-time dad has many benefits. If the wife is a career woman, her
10 husband can take some family responsibilities off her shoulders, **thereby** allowing her to compete more successfully in the workplace. The men share in the joy of participating in their children's day-to-day experiences. Differences in parenting styles between men and women are also believed to contribute to children's well-being. Studies suggest that a strong paternal[2] **presence** encourages greater curiosity, higher
15 self-esteem, and better emotional balance in the child. Societies with strong family units also report lower juvenile crime rates and lower rates of teen pregnancy. Robert Frank, a professor of child development at Oakton Community College in the U.S., notes that working mothers aren't necessarily **absent** from the home; many women form a close relationship with their kids regardless.

---

[1] The **breadwinner** is the person who supports a family with his or her earnings.
[2] The word **paternal** refers to anything related to the father.

20 In response to the recent increase in stay-at-home dads, new resources are becoming available. Playgroups are being planned for dads and their children. When Ryan Warren said that he felt out-of-place in groups that often consisted of all moms, his wife found a local group that hosted events for dads like Ryan and their children. "[My daughter] could play with other kids her age, and I could **hang out** with other fathers going

25 through the same experience," says Ryan. "In the group, we talk about the traditional guy things—sports, tools, cars."

Moving from a professional career to becoming an at-home parent is another challenge for these modern dads. But some men are finding ways to stay active with their career goals while 30 parenting at home. Dad and blogger Hunter Montgomery is a great example of a father who balances home life with career aspirations. "I was a full-time stay-at-home-dad, but I didn't plan it that way," says Hunter. "My **intention** 35 was to continue work as a mortgage loan officer from home; it's the type of work you can easily do remotely."

Hunter's wife, Christi, has a career in the U.S. Navy that sometimes requires the family to relocate. When Hunter and Christi had their first child, they already knew that they

40 would have to move within a year. To help with the **transition**, Hunter left his job to become a stay-at-home dad. Hunter was always interested in personal finances and, being home to watch the kids, he studied part-time to complete a master's degree in Family Financial Planning. Hunter started a blog, *Financially Consumed*, as a way to stay active in his career by sharing tips and experiences with others. Despite many

45 challenges, Hunter says he has found a way to balance both **priorities** of his family and his career. "All three of our kids are in school, and I have some time each day to pursue my interests," says Hunter. "I'm loving it."

It's safe to say that the stay-at-home dad is here to stay. As more and more dads find new ways to stay active socially and in their careers while parenting, they contribute

50 immensely to the flexibility of the father's role in the modern family.

A **Choose the correct answers for the following questions**

1 According to the passage, what did NOT change in the 1970s and 80s?
   a More women entered the workforce.
   b Many men decided to leave the workforce.
   c Men were encouraged to spend time with family.
2 How is having a stay-at-home dad said to benefit the child?
   a The child becomes more curious.
   b The child becomes more competitive.
   c The child is able to experience more things.
3 What does Ryan mean when he says he was looking to work *remotely* in line 37?
   a He has to work in an office.
   b He is able to work at home.
   c He is able to do his work at any time.
4 Which of the following is NOT true about Hunter Montgomery?
   a He writes a blog about being a stay-at-home dad.
   b His wife's job requires the family to move sometimes.
   c He completed a master's degree part-time.
5 What do Ryan and Hunter have in common as stay-at-home dads?
   a They can spend quality time with their children.
   b They can focus on maintaining their blogs.
   c They are members of their local playgroup.

B **Read the following sentences. Check (✓) whether they are true (T) or false (F).**

		T	F
1	Many people used to think that women should not be working.		
2	Robert Frank thinks career women are not close to their children.		
3	Ryan felt uncomfortable being in a playgroup full of women.		
4	Hunter wanted to be a full-time stay-at-home dad from the start.		
5	The Montgomery family had to move because of Hunter's job.		

C **Discuss the following questions with a partner.**

Critical Thinking

1 Are stay-at-home dads common in your country? Why, or why not?
2 How can governments help to ensure both parents spend enough time with their children?

Vocabulary Comprehension
Words in Context

A **Choose the best answer. The words in blue are from the reading.**

1   The sole person in the room is the _____.
    a   only person there   **b**   first person to arrive
2   Which involves some form of transition?
    a   reading a book   **b**   moving to a new country
3   Which word has the same meaning as *thereby*?
    a   thus   **b**   unlike
4   Which would be an example of having an intention?
    a   Luis is planning to go to art school.
    b   Luis graduated from art school.
5   When you are in someone's presence, you _____.
    a   are with the person   **b**   owe the person something
6   If something is a priority, it is very _____.
    a   exciting   **b**   important
7   Which is an example of hanging out?
    a   watching a movie with friends **b**   attending a wedding with family
8   Someone who is absent is _____.
    a   asleep   **b**   away

B **Answer the following questions, then discuss your answers with a partner. The words in blue are from the passage.**

1   What are some things you like to do when hanging out with friends?
2   In what way is the transition from childhood to adulthood challenging?
3   How do you behave in the presence of someone you dislike?
4   How do you think the sole survivor of a plane crash would feel?
5   Why is it important for students not to be absent from class too often?
6   What is the number one priority in your life now?
7   Think of an ending to this sentence: *Derek fixed my computer, thereby allowing me to ...*
8   What do you intend to do next weekend?

A Study the words in the chart. What do you think they mean? Match each word with a definition below. You may use a dictionary to help you.

Noun	Verb	Adjective
matriarch	—	matriarchal
maternity	to mother	maternal
patriarch	—	patriarchal
paternity	to father	paternal
juvenile	rejuvenate	juvenile

1 _____: the female leader of a family, usually the oldest or wisest
2 _____: motherhood (or pregnancy)
3 _____: to care for or nurture someone
4 _____: to feel refreshed again, usually after a rest
5 _____: related to fatherhood or being a father
6 _____: young; can also mean childish or immature
7 _____: the male leader of a family, usually the oldest or wisest
8 _____: related to the mother

B Answer the following questions, then discuss your answers with a partner.

1 What is the name of your maternal grandmother? How about your paternal grandfather?
2 At what age is one considered an adult and not a juvenile in your country?
3 Is maternity leave common in your country? How much time off work do women usually take?
4 Have you heard of the phrase *maternal instinct*? What do you think it means?
5 What is an activity that rejuvenates you?

Vocabulary Skill
The Root Words *pater*, *mater*, and *juv*

In this chapter, you read the adjectives *juvenile* and *paternal*. There are many words in English that begin with or include the root words *juv* meaning *young*, *pater/patri* meaning *father*, and *mater/matri* meaning *mother*.

Motivational Tip: Too challenging or too easy? Was the reading material in this chapter too challenging or too easy for you? In order to improve your reading abilities, you will need a combination of both. Challenging reading provides the opportunity to use effective reading strategies. Easier reading provides the opportunity to practice reading fluency.

Real Life Skill

Describing Family Relationships

In this unit, you've read about the changing family. In today's world, many people's families include more than their biological parents and siblings. There are some common names used to refer to these types of relatives.

A Match the following terms with the correct definition.

1 _____ mother/father-in-law
2 _____ ex-wife/husband
3 _____ step-brother/sister
4 _____ half brother/sister
5 _____ adopted child
6 _____ step-mother/father
7 _____ step-son/daughter

a another person's child legally made a member of your family

b a sibling related to you by marriage only

c your parent's spouse, but not your parent

d a child related to you by marriage only

e your spouse's parent

f your former spouse

g a sibling who shares the same mother or father as you

B Read the announcement below. Then use words from A to answer the questions. You might have to change the form of the word.

> **Hollywood Couple Announces Pregnancy**
>
> Actor Nicole Sommers is expecting a baby girl with husband Miguel Santiago in May. The happy couple have another child, Angelina, who was adopted a year ago. Ms. Sommers has a daughter from a previous marriage, Michelle (age 7) who is now living with her father, director Cameron DuBois. Mr. Santiago has twin boys, Alberto and Jorge, who live with his ex-wife. Ms. Sommers is currently shooting her latest film in the south of Spain.

1 Miguel Santiago is Michelle's _____.
2 Alberto and Jorge are Michelle's _____.
3 The new baby will be Jorge and Alberto's _____.
4 Miguel Santiago's father is Ms. Sommers's _____.
5 Alberto and Jorge are Nicole Sommers's _____.
6 Cameron DuBois is Ms. Sommers's _____.
7 Angelina is Michelle, Alberto, and Jorge's _____.

What do you think?

1 Do you think society has changed in the way it views the family or whether it considers strong family ties important? Explain your answer.
2 Do you think only children have different personalities than kids with siblings? Give an example.
3 Would you like for stay-at-home dads to become more common in the future? Why, or why not?

Fluency Strategy: SQ3R

SQ3R will help you be a better, more fluent reader and increase your reading comprehension. SQ3R stands for **S**urvey, **Q**uestion, **R**ead, **R**eview, **R**ecite.

Survey

Survey is similar to the A in the ACTIVE approach to reading; Activate prior knowledge. When you survey, you prepare yourself by skimming quickly through the text you will read. You read the title, the headings, and the first sentence in each section of the passage. You look for and read words that are written in bold or italics. Look at any pictures and read any captions. Through the survey, you prepare yourself to read.

Look at *Modern Fitness Trends* on the next page. Read the title and the first sentence in each of the seven paragraphs.

Question

After the survey, but before you read, ask yourself questions. "What do I want to learn as I read?"

Based on your survey of *Modern Fitness Trends*, write two or three questions that you hope to answer as you read.

1 _____

_____

2 _____

_____

3 _____

_____

Read

Following the survey and question stages of SQ3R, you read. You focus on comprehending the material. You move your eyes fluently through the material.

Read *Modern Fitness Trends*. As you read, keep in mind the 12 tips on pages 8 and 9. By combining those tips and SQ3R you will improve your reading fluency.

Modern Fitness Trends

Back in the 1980s, aerobics classes and leg-warmers (a type of sock that fits over the calves) were immensely popular. In the decade before that, bodybuilding was all the rage and Arnold Schwarzenegger was a huge icon for young men. The fitness world is always moving, and trends come and go very quickly. Here are three of the most popular fitness
5 trends right now. Which ones would you like to try?

If you love to dance and want to have fun with fitness, try Zumba.

Zumba is an immensely popular dance fitness program featuring Latin-inspired dance moves set to energetic music. It's
10 been called the "world's biggest fitness party" by its followers, with over 14 million people taking weekly classes, four million Zumba DVDs sold, and a line of "Zumbawear" clothing that has taken off.

15 The concept of Zumba came about by mistake, thanks to the quick thinking of a fitness instructor named Beto Perez. He was about to teach an aerobics class in his hometown of Cali, Colombia, when
20 he realized he had forgotten his aerobics dance music. He only had one cassette tape with him which was full of Latin music. "I improvised," he said, "and that was the beginning of Zumba." Instead of traditional dance-fitness classes where steps are counted
25 out loud to the beat of the music, Zumba has a free-flowing and party-like atmosphere. This proved popular with people who were fed up with working out, and Zumba moved from just another fitness fad to a true fitness phenomenon.

If you like intense activities and are up for a challenge, try CrossFit.

30 "No, it doesn't ever get any easier. You wouldn't want it to either." This quote by Greg Glassman, founder of CrossFit, says all you need to know about what some consider the most challenging fitness program ever.

Instead of featuring just one activity such as running or
35 weight-lifting, CrossFit tries to integrate gymnastics, track and field skills, and bodybuilding into a short and intense workout. A Workout of the Day (or WOD) may involve doing 20 pushups, followed by ten pull-ups, and then an 800 meter run—then repeating the set as many times as possible in 20
40 minutes. Because the workouts change every day, the body does not easily adapt and is always challenged. Of course, a danger is that some people go overboard and risk injury or, at the very least, suffer aches and pains for a few days. But for people who like to push the limits of fitness and strength—there are many police
45 officers, firefighters, and military people who follow it—CrossFit is the key.

If you prefer slower activities and want a good stretch, try Hot yoga

Most people think that yoga is all about
stretching. While stretching is indeed a
50 large part of yoga, it is also about creating balance in the body through strength and flexibility, and creating peace in the mind by forcing the person to concentrate on each pose. Hot yoga is seen as more challenging
55 compared to other forms of yoga, mostly because it's performed in a studio that is heated up to 40 degrees Celsius and with a high level of humidity. It may be a struggle at first to remain in the heated room for the
60 full class, but it gets easier over time!

While many yoga studios offer some form of hot yoga, the most popular is Bikram Yoga, named for its founder Bikram Choudhury. Each Bikram yoga class lasts 90 minutes and consists of 26 different poses. It is believed that doing yoga in a heated and humid room helps a person to stretch deeper and helps to prevent injuries. Choudhury also claims that
65 sweating will help cleanse the body of toxins and keep the internal organs in good health.

Review

After you read, you **review**. During the review stage of SQ3R you review the questions that you asked yourself prior to reading.

A   Did you find answers to your questions? Write the answers below.

1 _____

_____

2 _____

_____

3 _____

_____

Recite

The final step of SQ3R is to recite what you have learned while reading. The important thing is that you close your book and remember what you have read. You can recite in different ways.

- If you are alone, write down the key information that you learned as you were reading.
- If you have a partner, talk to him or her about what you have read.

Reading Comprehension

1 Why does the writer mention aerobics and bodybuilding in the first paragraph?
  a to introduce readers to more fitness options
  b to discuss future trends in fitness
  c to give examples of fitness trends over the years
  d to explain why the three trends featured are popular

2 In line 23, what does the word *improvise* mean?
  a to do something with little preparation
  b to make a mistake
  c to ask for assistance
  d to love to dance

3 Which of the following is true about Zumba?
  a It was the first dance fitness program.
  b It is not really considered a workout.
  c It was developed by the creator of aerobics.
  d You can do Zumba at home.

4 Which is the best example of a CrossFit WOD?
  a swimming the length of a pool as many times as possible for 20 minutes
  b skipping rope, lifting heavy weights, followed by sit-ups
  c doing a slow cross-country run for two hours
  d very intense stretching in a heated room

5 Why does the writer mention *police officers, firefighters, and military people* in lines 44–45?
  a CrossFit was actually created as training for them.
  b Only these people are fit enough to do CrossFit.
  c They are people who tend to prefer intense exercise.
  d They need to pass a CrossFit test to qualify for their jobs.

6 Which is NOT true about hot yoga?
  a It is usually done outside.
  b It is seen as a challenging form of yoga.
  c People may find the first class difficult.
  d People usually sweat a lot in class.

7 Who is most likely to believe exercise should be fun and social?
  a Arnold Schwarzenegger
  b Beto Perez
  c Greg Glassman
  d Bikram Choudhury

SELF CHECK

Write a short answer to each of the following questions.

1 Have you ever used the SQ3R method before?

  ☐ Yes   ☐ No   ☐ *I'm not sure.*

2 Do you think SQ3R is helpful? Why or why not?

  ☐ Yes   ☐ No   ☐ *I'm not sure.*

3 Will you practice SQ3R in your reading outside of English class?

  _____

  _____

4 Which of the six reading passages in units 7–9 did you enjoy most? Why?

  _____

  _____

5 Which of the six reading passages in units 7–9 was easiest? Which was most difficult? Why?

  _____

  _____

6 What have you read in English outside of class recently?

  _____

  _____

7 What distractions do you face when you read? What can you do to minimize those distractions?

  _____

  _____

8 How will you try to improve your reading fluency from now on?

  _____

  _____

Fluency Practice

Time yourself as you read through the passage. Write down your time, then answer the questions on page 169. After answering the questions, correct your responses and write down your score. Record your performance on the Reading Rate Chart on page 240.

SPACE TRAVEL AND SCIENCE FICTION

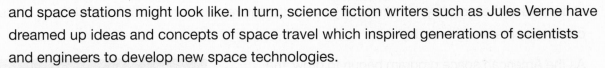

Space travel and science fiction have long been connected. Writers of science fiction, as well as creators of science fiction TV shows and movies, often study the latest scientific
5 concepts and use or adapt them to help portray what future space travel, space ships, and space stations might look like. In turn, science fiction writers such as Jules Verne have dreamed up ideas and concepts of space travel which inspired generations of scientists and engineers to develop new space technologies.

10 Jules Verne (1828–1905) was a French author and a pioneer of science fiction. In his novels *From the Earth to the Moon* (1865) and *Around the Moon* (1870), a kind of space ship is fired at the moon from a 900-foot-long cannon. At one point in their journey, the three travelers are deprived of gravity and float around their small ship. Rockets are used to slow the ship down before landing on the moon.

15 Given the time in which he was writing, Verne's predictions were very good. The size of his space ship was about the size of the first one to go to the moon, the *Apollo*, minus its large rockets. Both Verne's ship and the *Apollo* carried three people
20 into space. Furthermore, rockets were indeed used by the *Apollo* to slow its descent. However, Verne's ship shot his travelers into space, which never could have worked. The intense pressure of firing a

Apollo 11 begins its flight to the moon on July 16, 1969.

spaceship the way one would fire a bullet from a gun would cause
25 great physiological damage to the crew.

During the first half of the 20th century, science fiction novels
and comic books were very popular in the United States. Their
portrayal of space travel was less far-fetched than Verne's
and were often based on the space reseatch of that time. For
30 example, pictures began showing astronauts in space suits
when writers realized that exposing human beings to the cold,
airless environment of space was lethal. Ideas of other planets
were still often wrong, though. A 1928 drawing of a moon circling the planet Jupiter shows
it covered in plant life. It was only discovered later that the other planets and moons around
35 our sun are without life as we know it on Earth.

Drawings in the early 20th century also showed very large space ships and stations, almost like
floating cities. Writers at the time knew that trips to other stars would take hundreds of years.
Those who left Earth would die on the journey there, leaving their descendants to arrive at the
destination instead. Some writers addressed this problem by using the concept of suspended
40 animation—a deep sleep in which a person doesn't grow older. Such travelers would awaken
at the end of their journey, hundreds of years in the future. It is not impossible that these ideas
could become reality one day.

As the American space program begun to grow, the
television series *Star Trek* became very popular. The
45 series follows the adventures of a large space ship with
over 400 crew members that flies around the universe at
"warp speed," going faster than the speed of light. This is
a wonderful dream, but it will probably never be realized.
According to the current laws of physics, it is impossible
50 for any object to travel faster than the speed of light.

the space ship **USS Enterprise** from *Star Trek*

Science fiction has walked hand in hand with advances
in science and technology, and writers continue to study scientific concepts and to use
them to portray the future. Looking back at their ideas, some were correct and cannot be
distinguished from today's reality; many others were nothing but fiction. However, science
55 fiction writers continue to inspire new generations of people to dream of someday going
into space.

617 words   **Time taken** _____

Reading Comprehension

1 Which best summarizes the author's main idea?
- **a** Science fiction writers have been both right and wrong about the future of space travel.
- **b** The ideas of science fiction writers have caused scientists and engineers to make mistakes.
- **c** Science fiction writers will always be one step behind space research.
- **d** Scientists and engineers create inspiring science fiction that usually comes true.

2 *Given the time in which he was writing, Verne's predictions were very good.* (lines 15–16) Why does the writer say this?
- **a** Very little was known about space at that time.
- **b** Verne was known for making incorrect predictions.
- **c** Verne took a very short time to write his books.
- **d** Verne wrote the books at a very young age.

3 Which of the following predictions by Jules Verne was incorrect?
- **a** The first space ship would carry a crew of three people.
- **b** Space travelers would be deprived of gravity.
- **c** Rockets would be used to slow down a space ship.
- **d** A space ship would be launched using a very long gun.

4 Which fact about space travel was yet unknown to people in the early 20th century?
- **a** Humans were unable to survive in space without special suits.
- **b** The other stars in space were very far away from Earth and the sun.
- **c** Other planets in the solar system also had moons around them.
- **d** There was no plant or animal life on other planets in the solar system.

5 According to the passage, suspended animation was a concept used in science fiction to _____.
- **a** allow people to live longer
- **b** cure diseases
- **c** make time pass faster
- **d** help space ships travel faster

6 In line 48, what does the phrase *a wonderful dream* refer to?
- **a** the American space program
- **b** the television show *Star Trek*
- **c** traveling faster than the speed of light
- **d** a space ship with more than 400 crew members

7 Which could be another title for this passage?
- **a** A History of Space Travel
- **b** The Influence of Jules Verne
- **c** The Best Predictions in Science Fiction
- **d** Space Travel: Fiction and Reality

Fluency Practice

Time yourself as you read through the passage. Write down your time, then answer the questions on page 172. After answering the questions, correct your responses and write down your score. Record your performance on the Reading Rate Chart on page 240.

Single-Parent Families: Changing Views

The two-parent family is traditionally seen as the best way to raise children. In the past, single-parent families have had to deal with the stigma attached to their life choices. Nowadays, however, the single-parent family is the fastest growing type of family. Single parenthood can be the result of death, divorce, or separation, but it can also result from
5 single-parent adoption or women having children on their own thanks to fertility treaments. In the United States, a national survey showed that at least 50 percent of children, at some point in their childhood, will be members of a single-parent home.

Whether they elect to be single parents or have no choice, single parents are usually at a disadvantage in many ways compared to two-parent families. In a family with only one
10 breadwinner, money is often in short supply. Compared to homes where one parent is wholly dedicated to child rearing while the other works, children in single-parent homes receive less attention. Single parents can find themselves overwhelmed by their responsibilities both at work and at home.

15   There are some interesting statistics over the years concerning children of single parents. It's been well-documented that children from single-parent families have a slightly higher chance of becoming juvenile criminals. Other studies claim that these children are also more likely to drop out of school in their teens and to be jobless in their early 20s. A connection has even been made between children of single parents and higher rates of
20   obesity[1] and using illegal drugs.

Research has shown that there are certain factors that help single-parent families. One thing these successful families have in common is a strong support network, such as extended family, friends, or even special interest groups. Single parents need to remember that nobody
25   does it alone and there are many resources available to help them. For example, there may be government or non-profit organizations dedicated to helping single-parent families, or they can even turn to schools, community
30   centers, and religious organizations.

Single-parent families may even have certain advantages over two-parent families. Single parents have greater flexibility in spending time with children, because they don't have to take
35   the needs and schedule of a partner into consideration. Another advantage comes from the fact that single parents are more inclined to work together with their children to solve problems. This give-and-take between parents and children can make children feel more needed and valued, and give them a larger sense of responsibility.

It's important to mention the special challenges faced by the single father. Even today, when
40   the social and family roles of males and females are less defined than in the 50s and 60s, many people are reluctant to admit that men can be effective single parents. Modern men are more willing and able to cook and clean—responsibilities that were once exclusively assigned to women. Single fathers may also show more interest in the education and protection of their children, and report developing closer relationships as single parents.

45   Perhaps the most significant change is in society's attitudes towards single-parent families. There is much less discrimination both in terms of laws and how people view them. As single-parent families become more common, more and more people will start to view these family arrangements as normal. With enough community acceptance and support, the negative statistics linking single-parent families to youth crime and delinquency will definitely
50   improve. Single parents no longer have to fear whether their child(ren) will be treated differently from their peers.

---

[1] **Obesity** is defined as having an excessive amount of body fat, to the point where it affects one's health.

585 words   **Time taken** _____

Reading Comprehension

1 Which statement about single-parent families would the writer most likely agree with?
   a They are better than two-parent families.
   b They are unnatural and harmful to children.
   c They require extra support from the community.
   d They provide the best environment for raising children.

2 According to the first paragraph, why is it important that we leave behind the stigma attached to single-parent families?
   a because scientific fertility methods are growing
   b because the number of single-parent families is growing fast
   c because it is proven to be as natural as two-parent families
   d because single-parenthood can be the result of death or divorce

3 According to the passage, what is one positive thing that single parents can do?
   a get married
   b make time for themselves away from children
   c find support groups and understanding friends
   d dress their children in brand-name clothing

4 According to the passage, what advantage does a single-parent home have over a two-parent home?
   a Because they are more involved in problem solving, the children can feel more needed and valued.
   b Without two parents to control them, children grow up more naturally.
   c Single parents make more decisions for their children, so they make fewer mistakes.
   d Working single parents can train their children for a future career.

5 Which is an example of a challenge faced by a single father?
   a People think they are incapable of raising a child on their own.
   b They have problems bonding with their children.
   c They don't know how to cook and clean.
   d They are too busy to spend time with their children.

6 Why does the writer believe that the negative statistics about children of single-parent homes will disappear in the future?
   a There will be fewer and fewer single-parent families.
   b Single-parent families will become more fully accepted by society.
   c People will understand that there is a stigma attached to single-parent families.
   d Single parents will work much harder to educate and control their children.

7 Which could be another title for this passage?
   a Single-Parent Families: Facts and Statistics
   b The Problem of Single-Parent Families
   c Why Are There So Many Single-Parent Families?
   d Modern Perspectives on Single-Parent Families

The Future of Education

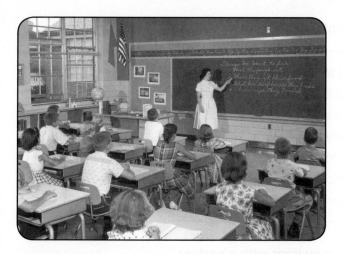

Discuss the following questions with a partner.

1　What are the students doing in the pictures above?
2　How do you think classrooms have changed in the last 50 years?
3　How do you think technology affects the way we study or learn?

Before You Read
Internet Survey

A Read the following sentences. Check (✓) the ones that apply to you.

> ❏ I use the Internet to do research on essay topics.
> ❏ I go online to find out more about a topic.
> ❏ I go online to find answers to questions.
> ❏ I discuss my studies on Internet forums.
> ❏ I write or have written a blog about my studies.
> ❏ I've done or am doing an online distance-learning course.
> ❏ I've handed in homework to my teacher online.

B Discuss the following questions with a partner.

1 Can you think of other ways you can use the Internet for your studies?
2 Do you think the Internet is a useful tool for studying? Why, or why not?

Reading Skill
Arguing For and Against a Topic

Many reading passages present two sides of an argument—one argues for the topic, presenting its strengths or its advantages; the other argues against it and presents its weaknesses or disadvantages. Words and phrases such as *but, however, though, in contrast,* and *in spite of* signal that an opposite or different opinion is about to be introduced.

A Skim the passage on the pages 175–176. Using information from the passage, write five advantages and disadvantages of learning online.

Advantages of Internet Learning

1 _____
2 _____
3 _____
4 _____
5 _____

Disadvantages of Internet Learning

1 _____
2 _____
3 _____
4 _____
5 _____

B Discuss your answers in A with a partner.

C Now read the entire passage carefully. Then answer the questions on page 177.

Internet Learning: The Future?

Internet Learning Set Me Free!
by Sam Tseng

When I was struggling with my chemistry class last semester, a professor suggested that I join a study group or get a tutor to **supplement** what we were studying in class. I couldn't afford a tutor and my schedule at university was so **erratic**—I couldn't arrange anything with classmates, especially ones I barely knew. Then a friend suggested going online. I can't believe I didn't think about it earlier! Online learning is perfect for me because it offers so much flexibility. Whenever I have free time, I can seek out lessons that revisit what my classes have been covering. And unlike being in class, I can pause the videos or watch them many times until I understand the concepts.

Another great thing about online lessons is that there are so many different educators out there, each with their own unique style and **perspective**. So if one teacher's approach doesn't work for you or you need a different viewpoint, you can always try another site. Each site also specializes in different subject areas. When I want to learn about a science or math concept, I visit the Khan Academy website, which explains topics using simple language and diagrams. For arts or philosophy, I go to TED-Ed, which offers lectures from experts all over the world. These sites have become so popular that **prestigious** universities like Harvard and Stanford have started offering free online courses as well.

I love online learning so much that I'm going to do a full online course offered by my university. I know that this requires an attention to deadlines that free lessons don't **entail**, but the freedom to work when I want will be so helpful when scheduling my other classes and getting a part-time job. Going online has opened up a whole new world for me—I think it's a trend that's here to stay.

Internet Learning Isn't for Everyone
by Jess Wachter

This spring I had an internship in Paris. Since I had time, I decided to take a couple of university courses online. I also looked for study material online to supplement my course, as recommended by a professor. At first, I found that resources online were plentiful and varied. However, I spent a lot of time locating lessons that offered **reliable** content, and for the specific topics I was searching for. When I did find classes with helpful material, I often felt there was something missing.

I soon realized that I was missing the teacher-student and student-student interactions of a conventional classroom and it was having a negative effect on my learning. I realized I learn best in a social environment with lots of opportunities for discussion. Studying on my own was boring and there were too many things to **distract** me online. I also didn't have the motivation or encouragement you get from teachers and classmates. Because I assumed I could study any time, I almost stopped studying completely until everything was due at the end of the semester! I think I'm the kind of person who needs the **pacing** and regular deadlines of a class.

To be fair, I certainly found material that was very helpful. But I was spending as much time on these lessons as I was on my own classwork and didn't have anything to show for it. I hear there are now online courses available where you can get your work marked by professors and be awarded a certificate if you pass. But I can't see people choosing to do these courses as a replacement for an actual university course and degree. It'll be a long time before employers and companies recognize such online credits[1] or degrees.

It's really great that quality education is being made available for free, but for me, online lessons probably work best as something extra to support my classroom experience.

---

[1] **Credits** measure the student workload required for the successful completion of a study program or qualification.

A **Choose the correct answer for the following questions.**

1 What will change when Sam does a full university course online?
  a He will have to keep to certain deadlines.
  b He will have to attend classroom sessions.
  c He will have to stop visiting sites like TED-Ed.
2 What does Jess admit is good about Internet learning?
  a She can study alone without any distractions.
  b She can study anytime she wants.
  c There are many helpful resources available.
3 What does *it* refer to in line 51?
  a the extra work Jess put in
  b Jess' classroom work
  c Jess' internship work
4 Why does Jess feel online credits or degrees aren't going to replace conventional ones?
  a She thinks employers won't recognize them
  b She thinks the education is not high quality enough.
  c She thinks the work won't be marked by real professors.
5 What is the overall message of the passage?
  a Online learning is the future of education.
  b Online learning will never replace the traditional classroom.
  c Online learning is great for certain kinds of people.

B **Read the following sentences. Check (✓) whether they are true (T) or false (F).**

		T	F
1	Both Sam and Jess currently have jobs or internships.		
2	Sam's professor recommended going online for help with his classes.		
3	Khan Academy is a good site for exploring chemistry topics.		
4	Sam prefers to study at his own pace.		
5	Jess prefers to have a structured schedule for her studies.		
6	Jess spent far less time on online lessons compared to her classwork.		

C **Discuss the following questions with a partner.**

Critical Thinking

1 What kind of personalities do you think Sam and Jess have? Who are you more similar to?
2 Are there some subjects that might be more difficult to study online than others? Which ones, and why?

Vocabulary Comprehension

Definitions

A Match the words in the box with the correct definitions. Write a–h. The words are from the passage.

a supplement	**b** erratic	**c** perspective	**d** distract
e prestigious	**f** entail	**g** reliable	**h** pacing

1 _____ point of view
2 _____ dependable
3 _____ having a very good reputation
4 _____ inconsistent; irregular
5 _____ to involve or include
6 _____ speed; rate of progress
7 _____ added to complete or extend something
8 _____ to draw attention away from your focus

B Complete the following sentences using the words from **A**. You might have to change the form of the word.

1 The job may be well-paid but it probably _____ staying late in the office.
2 My parents want me to be a lawyer or doctor because they consider them _____ occupations.
3 Many people _____ their diets by taking vitamins.
4 His behavior has been really _____ lately—he gets angry very easily and even shouts at people.
5 I can't study in public places as I find the noise very _____.
6 In Japan, trains are a(n) _____ mode of transport as they usually arrive on time.
7 It's important to try to understand a political issue from many different _____.
8 The _____ of the movie wasn't very good—the ending felt really rushed.

Motivational Tip: Reevaluate the comprehension quiz. Review each of your responses on the comprehension quiz. For the items you got correct, identify why you got them correct. For the items you got incorrect, identify reasons why you think you missed those questions. When you review questions you missed, you can identify your mistakes and learn from them.

A Look at the following words containing *ven/vent*. Write the part of speech and a simple definition. You may use a dictionary to help you. Discuss your ideas with a partner.

	Vocabulary	Part of Speech	Definition
1	conventional	*adjective*	*usual or traditional*
2	convene		
3	circumvent		
4	intervene		
5	avenue		
6	revenue		
7	prevention		

B Complete the following sentences using words from the chart in **A**. You might have to change the form of the word.

1 A common saying is that "_____ is better than cure." For example, it's better to keep healthy by exercising and eating well than to constantly visit the doctor.

2 A large crowd _____ in front of the university last week to hear the president speak.

3 Before Carl could hit Scott, Brett _____ and stopped the fight.

4 Thanks to a great sales team, the company has almost doubled its _____ this year.

5 In the United States, cigarette companies can't advertise on TV. However, many of these companies _____ this rule by advertising at sporting events that are televised.

6 If you walk up that _____, you'll be able to see his house.

C Can you think of any other words in English that include the root words *ven/vent*?

Vocabulary Skill
The Root Word *ven/vent*

In this chapter you read the adverb *conventional*, meaning *usual* or *traditional*. The noun form *convention* means *a large meeting of people*. Both words include the root word *ven* (sometimes also written as *vent*), meaning *to come*. For example, when you *invent* something, you come upon it for the first time, whereas a *venue* is a place to which people come, often for an event.

CHAPTER 2 Plagiarism and the Internet

Before You Read
The Great Technology Debate

A Some people feel using technology in the classroom has a negative effect on learners. Read the following ideas and, with a partner, come up with one positive and one negative point for each.

> using the Internet to do research
>
> typing homework or class notes instead of writing them by hand
>
> watching a video instead of listening to the teacher
>
> using a calculator to do math problems
>
> reading articles online rather than in a book

B Now get into two groups, one group representing the positive side and one representing the negative side. Choose the best points from each side and present them to the rest of the class.

Reading Skill
Identifying Meaning from Context

To guess the meaning of an important but unfamiliar word in a reading passage, try the following: First, think about how the new word is related to the topic of the reading. Second, identify what part of speech it is. Then look at the words surrounding the new word for synonyms, antonyms, or an explanation of the word.

A Read the following sentence from the article on the next page. Then answer the questions about the word in blue.

> While this kind of plagiarism usually happens innocently, it is still an offense.

1 The word offense is a(n) (verb / noun / adverb).
2 Offense probably refers to something (positive / negative).
3 In this sentence, offense probably means a(n) _____ .
   a crime   **b** upsetting event   **c** accident

B Look for the following words in blue. Read the sentence containing the word, and the surrounding sentences. Then choose the best definition.

1 In line 9, the phrase akin to probably means _____ .
   a different from   **b** the same as   **c** a result of
2 In line 19, the word well-meaning probably means _____ .
   a intending to do something wrong
   b understanding the meaning of something
   c having good intentions
3 In line 47, the word automatically probably means _____ .
   a independently   **b** quickly   **c** thoroughly

C Now read the entire article carefully. Then answer the questions on page 183.

Plagiarism and the Internet

The Internet is the largest library in the history of the world and a great resource for anyone seeking information. But doing research on the Internet is not without its risks. In recent years, plagiarism from online sources has become a serious problem, especially among students.

5　Original written work and information are protected by copyright laws, like original inventions. Therefore, when you reference or use information you find while doing research, you should always give credit to the person or organization that produced it. To plagiarize is to use ideas that are not your own without giving credit to the original source, or to claim that someone else's ideas are your own. It is **akin to** stealing

10　someone else's work. For example, if a student reads three articles and uses ideas from the articles to make his arguments in an essay without quoting or **citing** from the original work, the student is plagiarizing.

Internet-related plagiarism has become such a problem because it is so easy to find and copy information online. There are thousands of resources for students who

15　wish only to copy or **cheat**. However, the Internet also makes it easier for educators to check for plagiarism. Often a simple Internet search for a quote will be enough to expose copying. Some educators are more concerned about unintended plagiarism. Because copying and pasting is so easy, it is becoming more and more common for **well-meaning** students to mix up source material with their original ideas. While this

20　kind of plagiarism usually happens innocently, it is still an **offense.**

In addition to being a dishonest practice, plagiarism is a lost opportunity for students. The Yale College Writing Center, which is part of the prestigious Yale University in the United States, cautions, "If you paste in someone's words as your own, you will miss the opportunity to add your commentary, and therefore miss an opportunity to grow as

25　a thinker and writer." The practice of writing is to share one's own ideas and creative talent, but poor citation makes it unclear whether the writer is working out his own ideas or just playing with someone else's.

When working on a complex research assignment, managing your sources can
30 become challenging. Here are some tips to keep your sources in order and avoid plagiarizing:

- **Copy and paste important information.** The first step of researching is to gather
35 information. Be efficient and keep a computer document named "References" where you can keep useful information. Format the document so that each page starts with the citation, prepared in the format preferred by your professor, and then the important information you gathered from that source. Copy and paste the
40 material directly from the source.

- **Print out important articles.** When printing the whole document is not possible, print the first page of the article, which lists crucial details like the name of the writer and publication, and the date of publication. Then print pages that have the information you need and highlight the most important details.

45 - **Use software meant for managing sources.** Most universities and schools provide students with free or low-cost software that is designed to keep track of information. To save time, many programs will **automatically** format your citations so you don't have to type everything out yourself.

- **Insert citations into your drafts.** Most word processing programs have a
50 "comment" feature. This allows you to add notes throughout the document that aren't included in the document's word count and can be easily hidden. Every time you quote a source, type the source's citation into a comment box. This will save time when you have to compile everything into a bibliography.[1]

- **Double-check your work.** In the same way that you review your work for **clarity**
55 and mistakes, you need to check that you have matched the quoted information with the correct source.

---

[1] A **bibliography** is a list of source materials used in the preparation of a work or referred to in the text.

A **Choose the correct answer for the following questions.**

1   What is the purpose of this article?
   a   to warn students about plagiarism and explain how to avoid it
   b   to give readers a complete history of plagiarism
   c   to show that the Internet is making plagiarism worse
2   Which is NOT considered plagiarism?
   a   The student describes someone else's idea in his own words without giving credit.
   b   The student uses a quote from a book and forgets to mention the original source.
   c   The student cites a few authors, then arrives at his own conclusion about the topic.
3   Plagiarism is considered a "lost opportunity" because _____ .
   a   students will not be able to cite or reference properly
   b   students will never learn to develop ideas of their own
   c   teachers will never know if the students are cheating
4   Why does the author include tips in the article?
   a   to help students organize and manage their references
   b   to show students how to use a computer for their essays
   c   to encourage students to revise and edit their work

B **Answer the following questions using information from the passage.**

1   How do you define plagiarism?
   _____
   _____
2   Why is Internet plagiarism seen as a growing problem?
   _____
   _____
3   How can teachers use the Internet to check if a student has plagiarized?
   _____
   _____
4   How can computer software help students to avoid plagiarizing unintentionally?
   _____
   _____

C **Discuss the following questions with a partner.**

Critical Thinking

1   Is plagiarism a problem in your school or country? Why, or why not?
2   Do you think a student who accidentally plagiarizes should be punished? Why, or why not?

Vocabulary Comprehension
Words in Context

A **Choose the best answer. The words in blue are from the passage.**

1 A draft of an essay is one that is at _____.
   a an early stage   **b** the final stage

2 You cite a source in an essay to give _____ for an argument.
   a evidence   **b** your personal views

3 It is an offense for someone to smoke _____.
   a outdoors   **b** on a plane

4 When a door is automatic, it _____.
   a opens by itself   **b** needs to be unlocked

5 If I'm seeking greater clarity on something, I probably _____ it.
   a understand   **b** don't understand

6 Someone who cheats is known to be _____.
   a honest   **b** dishonest

7 Tasting food is akin to _____.
   a painting a picture   **b** smelling perfume

8 Which is an example of a person who is well-meaning?
   a someone who purposely gives advice which leads to bad results
   b someone who gives bad advice thinking that it is good

B **Answer the following questions, then discuss your answers with a partner. The words in blue are from the passage.**

1 Some people think downloading music on the Internet is akin to stealing. What do you think?

2 Do you think technology has made it easier to cheat in exams?

3 Can you give an example of something you did that was well-meaning but eventually went wrong?

4 Give an example of an offense.

5 What do you do automatically the moment you wake up?

6 What references might you cite when writing an essay on disease?

7 How many drafts of an essay do you normally write?

8 What should you do in order to write with clarity?

Motivational Tip: Review your reading fluency progress. Refer to the reading rate and reading comprehension charts at the end of the book. How would you evaluate your progress? Are you on a plateau? Are your scores gradually going up? Use these charts as a way to evaluate the progress you are making. What goals can you set for yourself as you continue in the next unit?

A Write the –*ism* forms of the following root words. Then discuss the meanings of each word with a partner. Use a dictionary to help you.

Word or Root	-*ism* form
1 critic	
2 mechanic	
3 sex	
4 patriot	
5 Buddha	
6 vegetarian	
7 race	
8 alcohol	

B Complete the following sentences with a word ending in –*ism* from **A**.

1 Hanging a national flag outside your house is one way to show your _____ .

2 Magicians use a box with a special _____ to allow them to hide from the audience.

3 I practice _____ because I don't believe in killing and eating animals.

4 _____ occurs when people judge others by the color of their skin.

5 _____ is a religion that is mainly practised in Asia.

6 When the company promoted a much more junior man above her, Lisa complained of _____ .

7 If you drink too much beer or wine, you can develop an addictive condition called _____ .

8 When a teacher gives students feedback on how their writing can be improved, that is a helpful form of _____ .

Vocabulary Skill
The Suffix -*ism*

In this chapter you learned the word *plagiarism*, which ends with the suffix -*ism*. The suffix -*ism* can indicate an action or process (e.g. *plagiarism*) or a state or condition (e.g. *optimism*). It can also be used to refer to a religious or political movement, or to indicate opposition to or intolerance of something (e.g. *ageism* means to discriminate against certain age groups, usually older people).

Real Life Skill
Identifying Common
Academic Abbreviations

There are many
common abbreviations
used to refer to
qualifications, or
academic degrees,
one receives after a
period of study. These
abbreviations are
written as well as said,
and when spoken,
each letter of the
abbreviation is usually
pronounced.

A Match each abbreviation with the correct definition.

Degree		Definition	
1	_____ BA	a	Master of Science
2	_____ BS/BSc	b	Master of Arts
3	_____ MA	c	Bachelor of Science
4	_____ MS/MSc	d	Doctor of Philosophy
5	_____ MEd	e	Master of Business Administration
6	_____ MBA	f	Bachelor of Arts
7	_____ PhD	g	Master of Education

B Complete the chart below with the correct abbreviations.

	A person who graduates from university with a...	is awarded a...
1	degree in biology	
2	degree in education, one level above a bachelor's	
3	degree in English	
4	degree in business, one level above a bachelor's	
5	degree in chemistry, one level above a bachelor's	
6	degree of the highest rank, above a master's	
7	higher degree in history, one level above a bachelor's	

C Discuss your answers in **B** with a partner. What kinds of degrees are common in your country? What degree do you intend to work towards?

What do you think?

1 Do you think online learning will eventually replace traditional schools and classrooms?
2 In addition to better organizational skills, what do you think can be done to help students avoid plagiarizing?
3 Do you know any famous cases of plagiarism? What happened in those cases?

The Mystery of Memory UNIT 11

How Good is Your Memory?

	Yes	No

1 Do you remember people's names after meeting them for the first time?   ☐ ☐

2 Do you remember important dates such as birthdays and anniversaries?   ☐ ☐

3 Do you remember what you did on your last birthday?   ☐ ☐

4 Do you usually remember where you put things?   ☐ ☐

5 Do you remember to pay bills on time?   ☐ ☐

6 Can you remember the last three movies you saw? Write them down.   ☐ ☐

_____

_____

_____

7 Can you remember the names of the last three books you read? Write them down.   ☐ ☐

_____

8 Do you remember what you studied in your last English class?

☐ ☐

If yes, what? _____

Getting Ready

A Complete the survey above. Discuss your answers with a partner.

B Based on your answers in the survey, do you think you have a good or bad memory?

CHAPTER 1 The Mysteries of Memory Loss

Before You Read
Memory Quiz

A How much do you know about the brain and memory? Answer the following questions.

1 Neuroscience is the study of _____.
   a human behavior   **b** the brain   **c** memory
2 Which of the following diseases involves memory loss?
   a diabetes   **b** anemia   **c** Alzheimer's
3 The size of the average human brain has _____ over the last 5,000 years.
   a increased   **b** decreased   **c** stayed the same
4 Research shows that in most cases, if you damage one part of your brain _____.
   a the other parts of your brain will keep functioning
   b the rest of your brain will be damaged as well
   c the brain will find a way to repair the damage

B Discuss your answers in **A** with a partner. Then check your answers at the bottom of page 190.

Reading Skill
Identifying Main Ideas within Paragraphs

Many paragraphs are constructed around a main idea. This idea is usually presented in a sentence within the paragraph, usually in the beginning or concluding sentence. Skimming and finding the main idea will increase your speed of reading and comprehension.

A Skim each paragraph of the passage on the pages 189–190. Then write the number of the paragraph (1–6) next to the correct main idea.

_____ Memories are classified as declarative or non-declarative.
_____ Doctors are always working to uncover new things about memory and the brain.
_____ The case of HM proves people who suffer damage to the hippocampus can still learn.
_____ Over time, scientists have had changing ideas about how the brain makes and uses memories.
_____ There are severe memory loss conditions that are still a mystery to people.
_____ EP and HM are exceptional cases of people with brain damage and memory loss.

B Discuss your answers in **A** with a partner. Underline the sentences in each paragraph that helped you find the answer.

C Now read the entire passage carefully. Then answer the questions on page 191.

The Mysteries of Memory Loss

1   Many people claim to have a bad memory, and it's true that we have trouble at times remembering where we put our house keys or recalling the names of people we've recently met. But there are

5   those who suffer more serious memory problems, including memory loss over time or memory loss due to injury, disease, or **complications** of surgery. These conditions are still not very well understood by doctors and scientists.

2   Many people experience memory loss as they age. In the past, neuroscientists—

10   doctors who study the brain—had theories about how the brain contained only a certain number of cells and how, over time, these cells might get used up. More recent research suggests that the brain may continue to manufacture new brain cells throughout a lifetime. Also, there is now evidence that damage to the hippocampus— an area of the brain thought to be important in the process of recalling information—

15   may play an important role in memory loss. Studies conducted on patients who have suffered damage to this area of the brain show that while they can still recall memories stored before the brain was damaged, they are unable to remember new facts. In addition, diseases associated with old age, (such as Alzheimer's,) and other problems involving short- and long-term memory loss, are now being **traced** to

20   possible damage to the hippocampus.

3   Two very special patients have helped doctors study memory and the hippocampus in recent years. These two men are referred to only as EP and HM, and each of them suffered memory loss after the loss of this particular section of the brain. HM suffered a head injury as a child and later underwent experimental brain surgery to remove

25   most of his hippocampus. EP, in contrast, contracted a disease that ate away much of his hippocampus. Both men are now unable to form new memories, but they can remember some things from before their traumas. For example, both EP and HM are likely to recall things they learned in school or family memories from their youth, but both will also always think it's the first time they've met you, **no matter** how many

30   times you may have met previously.

4 Through HM, who has been studied much longer than EP, researchers have learned about different memory abilities. Even though HM couldn't say what he'd had for breakfast or name the current U.S. President, there were some things that he could remember. Scientists found that he was able to learn complicated tasks without even
35 realizing it. In one study, he learned how to recreate a drawing by only seeing the drawing's **reflection** in a mirror. Each time HM did the task, he claimed never to have tried it before. And yet, each day his brain got better at guiding his hand to work in **reverse**.

5 Scientists generally **classify** memories into two categories: *declarative* and
40 *non-declarative*. Declarative memories are things you know you remember, like the color of your car or what happened yesterday afternoon. EP and HM have lost the ability to make new declarative memories. Non-declarative memories are the things you know without **consciously** doing them, like how to ride a bike or how to walk from your bed to your bathroom. Those unconscious memories don't rely on the hippocampus.
45 They happen in completely different parts of the brain. As EP and HM so **strikingly** demonstrate, you can damage one part of the brain and the rest will keep on working.

6 The exact process by which memories are coded and retrieved remains a mystery, but scientists and doctors are working to better understand the brain's remarkable ability to store and recall information.

Answers to Memory Quiz on page 188:
1. b; 2. c; 3. b; 4. a

A Choose the correct answers for the following questions.

1 It is considered a _____ for someone to occasionally forget names
or misplace their keys.
   a mystery
   b normal occurrence
   c major problem

2 Which is now thought to be true about brain cells?
   a They are limited in number.
   b They are constantly being renewed.
   c They are slowly used up over the years.

3 What can a patient with hippocampus damage remember?
   a the names of his father and mother
   b the name of the person he met an hour ago
   c what he ate for dinner the night before

4 Which is considered a non-declarative memory?
   a reciting a poem
   b catching a ball
   c recalling a phone number

5 Which is true about HM and his drawing task?
   a He can remember how to do the task.
   b He can do the task but can't remember that he can do it.
   c He remembers doing the task but can't remember how to do it.

**B Read the following sentences. Check (✓) whether they are true for HM
and/or EP.**

This patient...	HM	EP
1 suffered damage to the hippocampus.		
2 was unable to form new memories.		
3 contracted a disease.		
4 got a head injury when he was young.		
5 was studied for a longer time than the other.		

C Discuss the following questions with a partner.

Critical Thinking

1 Do you think it is possible for people like HM or EP to lead full lives?
   Why, or why not?
2 Why is it helpful or important to understand how the brain makes and
   uses memories?

Vocabulary Comprehension

Odd Word Out

A Circle the word or phrase that does not belong. The words in blue are from the passage.

1	solution	answer	complication	fix
2	no matter	despite	even though	however
3	classify	weaken	fade away	decline
4	aware	conscious	known	ignored
5	recall	connect	trace	link
6	source	origin	root	reflection
7	opposite	reverse	identical	other side
8	boring	shocking	striking	amazing

B Complete the following sentences with the words in blue from **A**. You might have to change the form of the word.

1 Even though they're not twins, it is _____ how similar the sisters look.

2 After her new haircut, Sally was shocked to see her _____ in the mirror.

3 _____ how much you plan ahead, there are always _____ when you move to a new house.

4 Scientists _____ animals into different groups and families.

5 We can't go any further in this direction, so put the car in _____ and back up.

6 Blinking and breathing are things we do without thinking; we aren't _____ of the fact that we're doing them.

7 By examining the crime scene for evidence, police can _____ the crime to the suspect.

Motivational Tip: Set a class goal. Together with your classmates, set a class goal for reading rate and reading comprehension for the next lesson in this unit. How many words-per-minute do you think your class can achieve? What level of comprehension can you achieve? At the end of this unit, check to see if you have met your class goals.

A Look at the chart below containing root words and their meanings.

Root word	Meaning
bene-	good, well
de-	not, away, down
magna-/magni-	great, large
pro-	forward
sign-	to mark, to mean
spec-	to see or look
sub-/suf-	under, beneath

Vocabulary Skill
The Root Word *fic/fice*

In this chapter you learned the word *sufficient*, meaning *enough*. This word is made by combining the root word *fic*, meaning *to do* or *to make*, with the prefix *suf-* and the suffix *-ent*. *Fic* or *fice* can be combined with other root words, prefixes, and suffixes. Verbs that end in *-fy* are related to the root *fic/fice*.

B Write the parts of speech for the words in the box below. Then, using the chart in **A** to help you, match the words to the correct definitions. Write a–j.

a _____ sufficient
b _____ beneficial
c _____ deficit
d _____ defy
e _____ insignificant
f _____ magnificent
g _____ magnify
h _____ proficient
i _____ specify
j _____ specification

1 _____ to make something appear larger, or to increase its effect
2 _____ too small to be important
3 _____ to refuse to follow orders or do something
4 _____ enough for a specific purpose
5 _____ a requirement which is clearly stated
6 _____ extremely good, beautiful, or impressive
7 _____ helpful or giving an advantage
8 _____ to mention or state in detail
9 _____ skilled in something
10 _____ the amount by which the actual sum is lower than what is expected

C Complete the following sentences using the words in the box from **B**.

1 I saw a (n)_____ exhibit at the Museum of Modern Art yesterday—some of the finest paintings I've ever seen.
2 Danny is _____ in several languages because he lived in many different countries when he was young.
3 Does the class syllabus _____ which unit we should read first?
4 In order to see a human cell properly, you'll need to _____ it.
5 The doctor recommended I take vitamin C because it's _____ to my health.

CHAPTER 2 Words to Remember

Before You Read
What Do You Remember?

A How good is your memory for the following things? Check (✓) the boxes that apply.

		Poor	So-so	Good	Excellent
1	people's names				
2	how to get to places				
3	people's faces				
4	telephone numbers				
5	meetings and appointments				
6	song lyrics				
7	the taste of foods				
8	vocabulary				

B Discuss your answers in **A** with a partner. Why do you think it is easier to remember some things than others? How do you think this affects the way you learn?

Reading Skill
Scanning

> When we need to find certain information in a text, we move our eyes quickly across the page. When we see part of the text that might have information we need, we read only that section. Scanning allows us to save time on tests, when searching for information on the Internet, etc.

A Read the following questions, then scan the passage on the pages 195–196 to find the answers. Write short answers.

1 How many methods of memory enhancement are outlined in the passage?

2 What is the meaning of the word *mnemonics* in line 11?

3 What images might be used to represent the word *tremendous*?

4 To use the loci method, what do you need to visualize?

5 When using the grouping method, what can you be creative about?

B Discuss your answers in **A** with a partner.

C Now read the entire passage carefully. Then answer the questions on page 197.

Words to Remember

How many English words do you need to know in order to be considered fluent? Experts disagree on the exact number of words learners need to know to achieve fluency in a new language, but

5 they generally agree that you need to know at least several thousand. Many language learners have at some point wished that they could simply insert a computer chip into their memories containing all

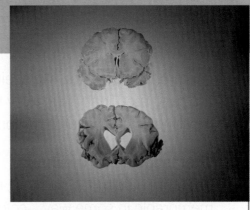

a disease-free brain (top) and a brain affected by Alzheimer's disease (bottom)

the vocabulary of the target language. Although that isn't yet **feasible**, with training, the

10 potential of the human memory can be unlocked. Many teachers suggest **accelerating** the vocabulary-building process by using mnemonics.

Simply put, mnemonics are methods used to help remember information that is otherwise difficult to recall. There are a wide variety of methods and different ones work better for different people, depending on their learning styles. The loci method is a primarily visual

15 system of remembering things. The association method encourages people to link target words to memorable images and utilize their senses. The grouping method works well for people who are good at linking concepts and organizing ideas together.

The loci method

This method is very useful for remembering lists of words. Before using this method,

20 it is necessary to **visualize** a path that you know well, such as the way to school or to work. Next, looking at your list of words, you'll need to create an image for each word, ideally one that is **vivid** and memorable. For example, for the word "accelerate," you might choose the image of a race car; an image for the word "enormous" might be a dinosaur. Creating these images may take a little practice. Then, imagine yourself

25 walking down your path and put the images you associated with the words at certain

common **landmarks,** like seeing a race car at the convenience store, a dinosaur in the park, etc. Finally, put away the list and move along the path in your mind again, recalling as many words as you can.

The association method

To commit a word to memory, it can help to associate it with an image that is memorable in some way—colorful, funny, embarrassing, beautiful, etc. For example, if you are trying to remember the meaning of the word "**tremendous,**" you might associate it with tremendously large trees and men. This image is connected to the word not only in meaning, but also in the sound of the first two syllables of the word. Say the word "tremendous", and you hear "tree" and "men." This pairing of meaning, sound, and images can help you memorize new words more quickly.

The grouping method

Try to memorize the following words: radio, pencil, index card, notebook, book, marker, magazine, newspaper, stereo, pen, MP3 player, paper. These words are meaningless on their own. But try dividing the list up into smaller groups (things you write with, things you write on, things you read, and things you listen to) and you'll probably find that you are able to **recollect** more words. When you encounter word lists that aren't so clearly divisible, you may need to be creative about categorizing the words.

What these three methods of memorization have in common is the idea of active learning. While it is certainly possible to **absorb** a great deal of information by just listening or reading, there is no guarantee that the information will remain in your memory in the future. We've looked at just a few of the many types of mnemonic devices that can be applied by language learners. In the end, it really depends on your own learning style and how you best retain information. Why not try a variety of methods and find the ones that work best for you?

A Choose the correct answers for the following questions.

1 What does the sentence *Many language learners . . . the target language* (lines 6–9) mean?
    a Many learners want to use the computer to learn vocabulary.
    b Many learners wish it was easier to learn vocabulary.
    c Our brains are like computers; memories are like computer chips.

2 Which statement about the loci method is NOT true?
    a You need to think about a path you are familiar with.
    b You need to be able to associate words with images.
    c You need to think about how to categorize words.

3 What is a potential problem with the grouping method?
    a Some word lists might be difficult to classify.
    b It may be hard to come up with striking images for words.
    c It may be hard to link syllables in the word to its meaning.

4 According to the article, how are these methods different from learning by listening or reading?
    a They require the learner to actively process words.
    b They help the learner to understand words better.
    c They encourage the learner to speak words more often.

5 What is another possible title for the article?
    a Why Memorizing Doesn't Work
    b The Future of Active Learning
    c Three Types of Mnemonics

B Read the following sentences. Check (✓) whether they are true (T) or false (F).

		T	F
1	Vocabulary is important in language learning.		
2	Most people have the potential to improve their memory.		
3	The association method encourages people to use their senses.		
4	The grouping method advises people to categorize items.		
5	Learning by reading and listening is a good way to remember things in the long-term.		
6	Not all mnemonic devices are suitable for all people.		

C Discuss the following questions with a partner.

Critical Thinking

1 Have you used any of these methods in the classroom? Would you want to be taught to use these methods? Why, or why not?

2 Do you know of other methods to remember vocabulary or study better?

Vocabulary Comprehension

Definitions

A **Match the words in the box to the following definitions. Write a–h. The words are from the passage.**

a vivid	**b** accelerate	**c** feasible	**d** absorb
e recollect	**f** landmark	**g** tremendous	**h** visualize

1 _____ a significant or outstanding feature in an area

2 _____ to remember

3 _____ bright, colorful, or intense

4 _____ to gain speed

5 _____ very great in amount or level

6 _____ able to be made, done, or achieved

7 _____ to form a picture in your mind

8 _____ to take in; to learn and understand

B **Complete the following sentences using the words from A. You might have to change the form of the word.**

1 There is _____ pressure on many high school students to study hard in order to get into a good university.

2 I love this painting because it uses such _____ color.

3 When the bathtub overflowed it took all the towels we had to _____ all the water.

4 Line graphs help us to _____ data trends over a period of time.

5 He has no _____ of what happened last night because he fell asleep.

6 For most of us, it's not _____ to memorize 100 new words in a day.

7 Franklin carries his language flash cards everywhere to help _____ his vocabulary learning.

8 If you get lost, look out for the public library. It's a big _____ in our town.

Motivational Tip: Reading for pleasure. As a class, discuss what you are reading because you want to read, not because you are assigned to read it. When you choose to make reading a regular part of your life, you will find greater levels of satisfaction, broaden your general knowledge, and improve your reading and writing skills.

A Review the different strategies you can use for associating and recalling vocabulary. Which do you commonly use?

Word Association: Linking one word to related words
e.g. school-related words: teacher, student, classroom, books

Synonyms and Antonyms
e.g. definite = certain; ≠ unsure

Word Families
e.g. attend, attention, attentive

Word Pairings (collocations)
e.g. hot coffee (not burning coffee)

Idioms
e.g. a last resort

Root Words, Prefixes, and Suffixes
e.g. the root *fic/fice*; the prefix *re-*

Mnemonic Aids
- Draw a picture that is related to the word or words.
- Relate the sound or spelling of the new word to a sound or spelling in your own language.
- Rhyme the new word with a similar word.
- Relate the words to furniture in a room or places in a city.
- Create a sentence or story using the words.
- Combine all the words to make an acronym (e.g. **ROY G. BIV** for the colors of the rainbow: **R**ed, **O**range, **Y**ellow, **G**reen, **B**lue, **I**ndigo, **V**iolet).

In this chapter, you read about three methods that people use for recalling new vocabulary. There are many different strategies that you can use to form associations between words in order to recall them more easily. You've already practiced some of these strategies in different chapters of this book.

B Use one or more of the strategies above to help you recall the words below. Share your strategies with a partner.

memory	memorize	accelerate	memorization
retention	short	mnemonic	active
short cut	recall	forget	beneficial
deficit	retrieve	device	long-term

Real Life Skill
Using Spelling Rules

In this unit, you've learned and reviewed some useful strategies for recalling vocabulary you learn in English. But what about spelling? Even though you can use the "spell check" feature on the computer, it is still helpful to be familiar with some of the basic rules for spelling in English. There are also several mnemonic aids you can use to recall the rules.

A Review some common spelling rules in English. Try saying each of the examples aloud.

Rule	Tip
IE or EI e.g. ceiling, neighbor, chief	I before E, except after C, or when sounded as A, as in *neighbor* and *weigh*.
Silent sounds e.g. mnemonic, psychology, debt, through	Circle or highlight the silent letter. Rhyme the word with another word (e.g. through – you, debt – jet) to remember pronunciation.
Dropping the final E e.g. care – caring, careful	Words ending in silent E: Drop the E if followed by a vowel (e.g. caring), but keep the E if followed by a consonant (careful).
Change Y to I e.g. beauty – beautiful	Usually, in words that end with Y after a consonant, drop the Y and change it to I before adding a suffix.
Doubling letters e.g. diner – dinner, stop – stopped	Often (but not always!) long vowels take one consonant: short vowels, two.

B For each pair, circle the word that is spelled correctly. Check your answers with a partner.

1 foreign   forin
2 wieght   weight
3 though   thow
4 recieve   receive

5 timeing   timing
6 accommodate   accommodate
7 sunnyest   sunniest
8 runing   running

What do you think?

1 How do you help yourself remember important tasks each day?
2 In what ways do you think human memory is different from computer memory? Are there any ways in which it is the same?
3 What do you understand by the term "active learning"? Can you think of other ways you can implement active learning in your English studies?

Getting Ready

Discuss the following questions with a partner.

1 Can you name any of the superheroes in the comics above? What superpowers do they have?

2 Why do you think these superheroes and their accompanying comics have remained so popular over the years?

3 Do you have a favorite superhero? Why do you like that hero?

CHAPTER 1 The Evolution of Batman

Before You Read
Batman Quiz

A Complete the following sentences about Batman.

1 Batman's crime-fighting partner is (Robin / Bane).
2 Batman uses the (Batmobile / Batarang) to get from place to place.
3 The police chief of (Metropolis / Gotham City) sometimes calls for Batman's help by using the (Bat Call / Bat Signal).
4 Out of costume, Batman is known as (Bruce Wayne / Peter Parker).
5 The Joker and (Lex Luthor / Ra's Al Ghul) are some of Batman's enemies.

B Discuss your answers with a partner.

Reading Skill
Recognizing Sequence of Events

> Sequence markers are words and phrases that signal to the reader the order of events in a passage. Expressions such as *then*, *soon after that*, *subsequently*, as well as days, dates, and times can act as sequence markers. The past perfect tense can also signal the order of events.

A Read the following sentences from the passage on the pages 203–204. Without reading the passage, put the events in order from 1–6. Circle the words in the sentences that helped you choose the order.

	In the latest Batman films, the hero's transformation continues in this direction.
	Not long after the creation of Batman, World War II began and the American government spent lots of time and energy getting its people to be patriotic and to support the war.
	The mood in America relaxed considerably by the 1960s, and a Batman show subsequently appeared on television with a very different kind of superhero.
	In the 1970s and 80s, Batman was embraced by comic book writers and re-imagined as a more serious character.
	Batman was created in 1939 by artist Robert Kane, who was inspired by crime novels, another comic character called Zorro, and an earlier horror film called *The Bat*.
	Batman returned to the big screen in 1989 in Tim Burton's *Batman*.

B Discuss your answers with a partner. Then skim the passage to check whether your answers in **A** are correct.

C Read the entire passage carefully. Then answer the questions on page 205.

The Evolution of Batman

The Dark Knight—one nickname for Batman—is a name that's layered with meaning. Batman is a classic superhero, but the modern day Batman is a far more complex character than he was 70 years ago. Over time, he has evolved from an **invincible** crime fighter into one of the most "human" superheroes, one who is often faced with dilemmas that challenge his morals and
5 conscience. The nickname "Dark Knight" fits the character we know today because Batman is always in pursuit of justice, but finds that difficult sacrifices must often be made along the way.

Batman was created in 1939 by artist Robert Kane, who was inspired by crime novels, another comic character called Zorro, and an earlier horror
10 film called *The Bat*. Because Kane preferred more realistic heroes, Batman was not given superpowers. Instead, Bruce Wayne (Batman's alter ego[1]) is extremely rich and can afford many useful tools and weapons, such as the Batmobile,
15 a car with special capabilities. Batman's original suit and iconic "bat signal" have **endured** as well. While the design and colors have changed gradually over time, the Batman identity—bat logo,

Christian Bale as Bruce Wayne/Batman

mask with ears, cape—has been remarkably consistent for more than 70 years.

20 One thing that hasn't remained so similar over the years is the **tone** of the Batman stories and, accordingly, Batman's personality. The **conflicts** in Batman stories are often based on real-world problems, which is one element that makes Batman a more complex character than most superheroes. Not long after the creation of Batman, World War II began. The American government spent lots of time and energy getting its people to be **patriotic** and to support the
25 war. Batman appeared in a 15-part serialized movie at this time and was seen as a symbol of justice, fighting evil at home while American soldiers were away defending the country. At that time, he sometimes used guns and wasn't afraid to kill his enemies if there was a need to, but the modern Batman is generally against guns and killing because his parents were killed by guns.

The mood in the United States relaxed considerably by the 1960s, and a Batman show
30 subsequently appeared on television with a very different kind of superhero. The show became popular with kids and adults alike for its cultural references, cartoonish fight scenes, and funny

---

[1] **Alter ego** is a Latin phrase that refers to the second self or another side of oneself.

dialog. Following the end of the original television series in 1968, the television version of Batman was limited to cartoons for the next two decades.

35 In the 1970s and 80s, Batman was **embraced** by comic book writers and re-imagined as a more serious character. When legendary comics writers like Frank Miller and Alan Moore began to write Batman books, the Batman we know today—darker, imperfect, vulnerable—began to **emerge**. Miller is often credited with taking the comics genre to a 40 new level with his Batman book *The Dark Knight Returns*, which was among the first to incorporate real-world elements such as corrupt politicians and poverty. In his hands, Batman went beyond being just a masked hero.

Adam West and Burt Ward as Batman and Robin in the 1960s TV show

a movie poster for Christopher Nolan's *The Dark Knight*, featuring the Joker

Batman returned to the big screen in 1989 in Tim Burton's *Batman*. It 45 featured a tougher Batman, with a colder personality and a redesigned, all-black costume. In the latest Batman films, the hero's transformation continues in this direction. Christopher Nolan's *Dark Knight* trilogy[2] features a much more dangerous Gotham City and Bruce Wayne/Batman 50 are not automatically likable characters. Batman no longer simply fights against "bad guys," but starts to question if he's a good guy or hero himself. Villains like the Joker are no longer crazy personalities with weird hair and makeup that just want to rob a bank or kidnap a famous person; they are 55 now similar to modernday terrorists, trying to make people fight one another and threatening the world economy.

What makes Batman a great character is that he changes as the world changes. So while it is safe to expect that Batman will be a different character in 20 years' time, we can also expect that he will continue to be a 60 great and **compelling** superhero.

---

[2] A **trilogy** is a series of three related works.

A Read the following sentences. Check (✓) whether they are true (T) or false (F).

		T	F
1	Batman was partly based on a crime novel called *The Bat.*		
2	Batman doesn't believe in using guns because so many people died in World War II.		
3	The current movie version of Batman is more serious than the television version in the 1960s.		
4	Comic book writers were the first to incorporate real-world issues into Batman stories.		
5	Tim Burton directed the latest Batman movies.		
6	Batman becomes a bad guy in later Batman movies.		

B Answer the following questions with information from the passage.

1 What was Batman given in place of superpowers?

_____

_____

2 What was the character of Batman like during World War II?

_____

_____

3 What things about Batman have changed over time?

_____

_____

4 What things about Batman have stayed the same over time?

_____

_____

Critical Thinking

C Discuss the following questions with a partner.

1 Do you know of other superheroes or fictional characters that have changed over time? Give some examples.
2 Do you prefer superheroes to be complex and serious like modern-day Batman, or more like simple cartoon characters? Why?

Motivational Tip: Sit in a different seat today. In most classrooms, students sit in the same seat near their friends. Today, the challenge is to sit in a different seat next to someone you don't know very well. During today's class, when invited by your teacher, share what you are learning from today's reading with a new partner.

Vocabulary Comprehension
Words in Context

A **Choose the best answer. The words in blue are from the passage.**

1 Which describes the tone of an article?
   a lengthy
   b argumentative

2 Which of these is a conflict?
   a an argument
   b an agreement

3 When you embrace something, you _____ it.
   a reject
   b welcome

4 Her argument was so compelling that I _____ her.
   a believed
   b did not believe

5 The artist's work has endured because it _____.
   a is appealing to people of all ages
   b dealt with subjects that were specific to his time

6 Someone who is patriotic _____ his home country.
   a loves
   b hates

7 When you emerge from a shower, you are _____.
   a clean
   b dirty

8 The rugby player felt invincible during the game, as though _____.
   a he couldn't do anything
   b no one could stop him

B **Answer the following questions, then discuss your answers with a partner. The words in blue are from the passage.**

1 What tone of voice do you use when talking to young children?
2 How do you usually resolve conflicts with friends?
3 What new technologies have you embraced in recent years?
4 Do you know any superheroes who are invincible?
5 What things make you feel patriotic?
6 Are there any emerging actors or musicians that you like?
7 What do you think is the most compelling reason to learn English?
8 Do you know any famous figures who have endured hardships before becoming successful?

A Look at how compound adjectives are formed.

Some compound adjectives are formed by joining two words to form another word.

> *an outspoken man   a secondhand car   superhero*

Other compound adjectives can be formed by combining two or more words using hyphens. These usually appear before nouns.

> *Is Yuri Gagarin well known in your country? Is he a well-known astronaut? Karina's daughter is five years old. Karina has a five-year-old daughter.*

Some compound adjectives are fixed—the word order is always the same, and they are always hyphenated.

> *He's a self-confident guy.   He has a know-it-all attitude.*

B Complete the following sentences with the correct compound adjectives. Write a simple definition for each.

> up-to-the-minute   over-the-counter   out-of-the-way
>
> matter-of-fact   middle-aged

1 In order to have some privacy, Erik and Laura stayed at a(n) _____ hotel in the Colorado mountains.

Definition: _____

_____

2 If you want _____ information on the election results, tune in to channel 4.

Definition: _____

_____

3 I don't know exactly what the robber looked like; he had grayish hair and appeared to be _____ .

Definition: _____

_____

4 In the United States, you can't buy medicine such as antibiotics _____ . You can only get them with a prescription.

Definition: _____

_____

5 Antonio talked about failing his test in a very _____ way; it didn't seem to bother him at all.

Definition: _____

_____

C Now write three sentences using any of the compound adjectives you have learned. Discuss your ideas with a partner.

Vocabulary Skill
Compound Adjectives

> In this chapter, you learned the compound adjective *real-world*. Compound adjectives are formed when two or more nouns, adjectives, adverbs, or the participle form of a verb (e.g. *dressed*, *looking*) are combined to modify a noun.

CHAPTER 2 Graphic Novels Come to Life

Before You Read
Graphic Novels

A Answer the following questions.

1 Have you watched any of the movies above? What do they have in common?

2 Have you heard of the term *graphic novel*? What do you think it means?

B Discuss your answers with a partner.

Reading Skill
Identifying Main and Supporting Ideas

Most paragraphs have a main idea, or topic, that tells us what that paragraph is about. Often, you will find the main idea talked about in the first or second sentence of a paragraph. Supporting ideas usually follow the main idea. Sentences containing supporting ideas explain or give us more information about the main idea.

A Read the following sentences from the passage on the pages 209–210. Write *M* next to the main idea of the paragraph and *S* next to the supporting idea.

Paragraph 2

1 _____ The term "graphic novel" became popular in the 1980s when people wanted to distinguish between the colorful comic books aimed at kids and more complex stories aimed at older, more mature readers.

2 _____ While classic comic books feature crime-fighting superheroes, graphic novels cover many genres and are frequently about real-life issues.

Paragraph 3

3 _____ *Watchmen* was a box office hit, earning more than $180 million around the world.

4 _____ *Watchmen* by Alan Moore and Dave Gibbons is a great example of a graphic novel that has been successfully adapted for film.

Paragraph 4

5 _____ Authors are able to take risks in graphic novels that directors are unable to pull off believably on screen.

6 _____ Taking a graphic novel off the page and on to the screen isn't as simple as it sounds.

B Discuss your answers with a partner. Then skim the passage to check your answers.

C Now read the entire passage carefully. Then answer the questions on page 211.

Graphic Novels Come to Life

1 Superhero movies based on comic books have long been good business for Hollywood. Some of the most successful superhero movies, like *The Avengers* (2012), *The Dark Knight* (2008), and *Spiderman* (2002) have earned upwards of $400 million each at the box office. The appeal of superhero movies is obvious: it brings familiar and well-loved characters to

5 audiences, and these long-running comic series can easily be extended into movie **sequels**. Thanks to the success of these movies, more serious comic books such as graphic novels have also been adapted for the big screen.

2 The term "graphic novel" became popular in the 1980s when people wanted to distinguish between the colorful comic books aimed at kids and more complex stories

10 aimed at older, more mature readers. While classic comic books feature crime-fighting superheroes, graphic novels cover many genres and are frequently about real-life issues. *Ghost World* by Daniel Clowes, which follows two friends through the summer after their high school graduation, is an early example of a graphic novel that was made into a film. Another recent graphic novel adaptation is Marjane Satrapi's *Persepolis*, which

15 documents her youth in Iran during and after the Islamic revolution of 1979.

3 *Watchmen* by Alan Moore and Dave Gibbons is a great example of a graphic novel that has been successfully adapted for film. The only graphic novel to appear in *Time* magazine's list of the best 100 books since 1923, *Watchmen* was also a box office hit,

20 earning more than $180 million around the world. Director Zack Snyder says movies based on graphic novels appeal to movie audiences because they are deep, vivid stories. "*Watchmen* is thick and complicated and violent and political and critical of America," Snyder says. "It's huge."

4 25 But taking a graphic novel off the page and on to the screen isn't as simple as it sounds. The most challenging part for screenwriters and directors is attempting to make a movie that **deviates** from the original. Authors are able to take risks in

Watchmen director Zack Snyder

graphic novels that directors are unable **to pull off** believably on screen. For example,
30   *Watchmen* was considered "unfilmable" by many, including the writer Alan Moore
himself, because of the many different plot lines and time frames. While changes may
make the story more appealing to **mainstream** audiences, fans of the original material
are important and **unrelenting** critics. Snyder remarked, "The geeks will be on me for
changes I make to *Watchmen*. There are no more fierce fans than geekdom."

5   35   Risks aside, one major appeal of graphic novels for movie studios is that the visual
format allows them to "see" what the movie could look like before they approve it. This
can be a great advantage over a traditional script, which requires the reader to imagine
the characters and setting. Having a pre-defined style has also led to the creation of
some very unique movies. Two great examples of graphic novels that had their style
40   translated to the screen are Frank Miller's *Sin City* and *300*. The film adaptation of *Sin
City* **retains** the original story's dark look and feel because the directors—Miller and
Robert Rodriguez—shot it in a shadowy black and white style with only certain colors
allowed, such as the bright yellow of the main villain.

6   Turning a hand-drawn comic into a live-action film can be tricky, and directors must
45   attempt to create scenes with the same **intricate** detail as in the graphic novel, often
on a tight budget. For *300*, Snyder had to use special color filters and other techniques,
such as speeding up or slowing down the action, to help **convey** the action and bloody
violence of the book. By Hollywood standards, the $60 million budget that Snyder had
to work with isn't a lot of money, but as such movies continue to wow audiences and
50   make money, production budgets are sure to rise. Maybe your favorite graphic novel
will soon be coming to a screen near you!

a scene from *Sin City* the movie (left) and the comic (right)

A Choose the correct answer for the following questions.

1 The reading passage is about _____.
   a how comics are different from graphic novels
   b how graphic novels have come to be adapted into movies
   c why comics and graphic novels are worthwhile entertainment

2 According to the passage, which is NOT a difference between comics and graphic novels?
   a Comics are usually about superheroes; graphic novels are about real-life issues.
   b Graphic novels have older and more mature readers compared to comics.
   c Graphic novels have fewer images and drawings compared to comics.

3 The writer uses *Ghost World* and *Persepolis* as examples of _____.
   a how graphic novels can be about real-life issues
   b graphic novels that came out in the 1980s
   c how graphic novel adaptations make lots of money at the box office

4 The *geeks* in Zack Snyder's quote in lines 33–34 refers to _____.
   a fans of the graphic novel
   b the mainstream audience
   c professional movie critics

5 The purpose of paragraphs 5 and 6 is to _____.
   a show that *Sin City* was easier to direct compared to *300*
   b compare and contrast Frank Miller's graphic novels
   c show how the visual format can be both helpful and difficult for directors

B Read the following sentences. Check (✓) whether they are true (T) or false (F).

		T	F
1	Hollywood has only recently been adapting comics into movies.		
2	The graphic novel *Watchmen* is highly regarded by book critics.		
3	The writer of *Watchmen* did not believe it could be made into a film.		
4	Movie studios prefer traditional scripts to more visual scripts.		
5	A budget of $60 million is considered a lot of money for a Hollywood film.		
6	There will probably be more movie adaptations of graphic novels in the future.		

Critical Thinking

C Discuss the following questions with a partner.

1 Do you think there are things that can be shown in graphic novels that can't be shown on screen? Give some examples.

2 Some people don't consider comics or graphic novels to be serious books or literature. Do you agree? Why, or why not?

Vocabulary Comprehension

Odd Word Out

A (Circle) the word or phrase that does not belong in each group. The words in blue are from the reading.

1	sequel	chapter	series	actor
2	finish	finalize	convey	conclude
3	reserve	keep	hold	deviate
4	fail	pull off	achieve	accomplish
5	mainstream	unique	popular	common
6	unrelenting	tough	hard	incomplete
7	release	retain	remember	recall
8	intricate	detailed	plain	complicated

B Complete the following sentences using the words in blue from **A**. You might have to change the form of the word.

1 A drawing with such _____ details must have taken the artist a long time to create.

2 The radio tends to play more _____ music—songs that will appeal to many people.

3 She finds it hard to _____ her ideas in English because it's her second language.

4 The athletes had to train out in the open field despite the _____ heat of the summer.

5 The new edition of the book still _____ the old illustrations.

6 People still don't know how David Copperfield, a famous magician, managed to _____ the trick of making an airplane disappear.

7 It's better not to _____ from the recipe in case the cake comes out badly.

8 This is my favorite movie, but I hope they don't try to make a _____ ; some stories are good enough on their own.

A Complete the chart below using the antonyms in the box.

long-running deep simple unrealistic disgusting mature

Word	Antonym
juvenile	
intricate	
superficial	
true-to-life	
short-lived	
appealing	

Vocabulary Skill
Antonyms

An antonym is a word or phrase that has the opposite meaning of another word or phrase. One way of increasing your vocabulary is by learning antonyms.

B Complete the following paragraphs using the words from the chart in **A**. Not all the words will be used. Discuss your answers with a partner.

I'm not a fan of comic books or superheroes like Superman and Batman. For one, I find comics quite **(1)** _____; they're meant for children! I also find them completely **(2)** _____, since normal people don't have superpowers and there aren't villains running around trying to take over the world in real life! I think people's interest in comics and superhero movies is **(3)** _____ and just another fad.

I disagree. Comic books are for all ages, whether they are **(4)** _____ and colorful superhero ones meant for kids, or more **(5)** _____ graphic novels. Comics are great for visual people who appreciate the **(6)** _____ artwork. The format is very **(7)** _____ to me. I grew up reading comics and am still following some of the **(8)** _____ ones, which means I get to see the characters develop over a period of time. I think comics are popular because they discuss issues that are **(9)** _____ and relevant to us.

Real Life Skill

Reading Online Movie Reviews

A great deal of information is available about movies on the Internet. There are reviews of every popular movie ever made, both new and old. The Internet again proves itself to be a useful research tool.

A Think of two movies and find reviews for them online. Use the title of the movie plus "review" as keywords for your search.

B Scan the websites you found for information to complete the charts.

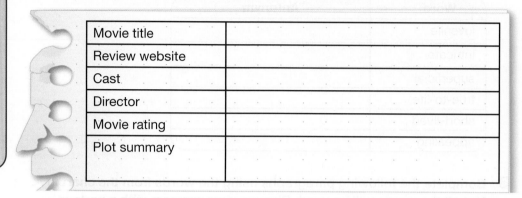

Movie title	
Review website	
Cast	
Director	
Movie rating	
Plot summary	

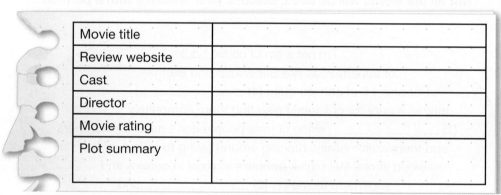

Movie title	
Review website	
Cast	
Director	
Movie rating	
Plot summary	

C Share the information you found with a partner.

Motivational Tip: How can this be applied beyond the textbook? Reading is a very important life skill that people use every day to accomplish real life tasks. How do the Real Life Skill sections in this book help you in everyday life? For example, being able to research and read movie information can help you find new movies or give ideas about movies you've already seen.

What do you think?

1 Batman and Bruce Wayne are the same person. Can you think of more superheroes with alter egos? Why do you think many superheroes have alter egos?

2 If you could have any superpower, what would it be and why?

3 Do you like Hollywood movies about superheroes? Why, or why not?

Fluency Strategy: Thinking ACTIVEly While Reading

In order to become a more fluent reader, remember to follow the six points of the **ACTIVE** approach—before, while, and after you read. See the inside front cover for more information on the **ACTIVE** approach.

Activate Prior Knowledge

Before you read, it's important to think about what you already know about the topic, and what you want to get out of the text.

A Look at the passage on page 217. Read only the title and look at the pictures. What do you think the article is about? What is homeschooling? Why might it be a better way to learn?

B Now read the first paragraph of the passage. What is the public education system like in your country? How did people used to be educated? Can you think of any countries where its people may not have faith in the public education system? Discuss with a partner.

Cultivate Vocabulary

As you read, you may come across unknown words. Remember, you don't need to understand all the words to understand the meaning of the passage. Skip the unknown words for now, or guess at their meaning and come back to them later. Note useful new vocabulary in your vocabulary notebook—see page 6 for more advice on vocabulary.

A Read the first paragraph of the passage again. (Circle) any words or phrases you don't know. Can you understand the rest of the paragraph even if you don't understand those items?

B Write the unknown words here. Without using a dictionary, try to guess their meaning. Use the words around the unknown word and any prefixes, suffixes, or word roots to help you.

New word/phrase	I think it means

Think About Meaning

As you read, think about what you can infer, or "read between the lines," such as the author's intention, attitude, and purpose for writing.

Skim the passage by reading the first and last paragraphs, and the first line of the other paragraphs. Then discuss these questions with a partner.

- Who do you think this article was written by?
- Who do you think will be interested in this article?
- Why do you think the writer is interested in this topic?
- What does the author mean by "mainstream education system"?
- Who do you think practices homeschooling?

Increase Reading Fluency

To increase your reading fluency, it's important to monitor your own reading habits as you read. Look again at the tips on page 8. As you read, follow these tips.

Now read the whole passage *Homeschooling: A Better Way to Learn?* As you read, check your predictions from *Think About Meaning*.

HOME SCHOOLING

A Better Way to Learn?

1 It is easy to forget that public education is a relatively new phenomenon. Even in the U.S., which has a relatively developed education system, public schools only started flourishing in the early 19th century. Before that, while the affluent were able to hire tutors for their children, most education of children took place within the family and the community. Some people are now
5 going back to teaching children themselves (or hiring tutors), especially in countries where the mainstream education system is considered poor.

2 The laws regarding homeschooling can be complex and vary widely from country to country. In some countries, such as France, England, Indonesia, and the United States, homeschooling is permitted by law. In other countries like Japan or Spain, laws are not so clear; homeschooling
10 goes on but isn't formally permitted by existing laws. Other countries, including Germany and Brazil, ban homeschooling altogether.

3 At one time, there was a stigma associated with homeschooling because it was traditionally for students who had behavioral or learning difficulties and could not keep up with the rest of the class. Today, there are many compelling arguments for educating one's children at home.
15 Some of it stems from dissatisfaction with the mainstream education system. Teacher shortages and lack of funding mean that, in many schools, one teacher is responsible for 30 or 40 pupils; children are often deprived of the attention they need. Bullying and increasing classroom violence have also motivated some parents to remove their children from school. Parents may also choose to homeschool for religious or political reasons.

4 20 Many psychologists see the home as the most natural learning environment, since it is supportive and has no distractions. Parents who homeschool say they can monitor their children's education more closely. Children
25 can also choose what and when to study, thus enabling them to learn at their own pace. The many educational resources on the Internet can also be used to supplement learning. Advocates of homeschooling point out that homeschooled
30 children do just as well or better than those who are classroom-taught, and a striking number gain admission to prestigious universities.

5 In contrast, critics of homeschooling say that children miss out on learning important social skills because they have little interaction with their peers. This might have a negative effect on
35 them later in life when they go to university or start work. Critics have also raised concerns about whether parents are capable of educating their child properly. Many of these parents lack teacher training and may not be competent or up-to-date on all the subjects taught in schools.

6 In the U.S., with an increasing number of parents taking their children out of class, school officials are looking for ways to restore parents' confidence in the public education system. Some American high schools have opened their doors to homeschoolers on a part-time basis, allowing these children to attend classes once or twice a week, or to take part in activities such as playing football or doing ballet. This enables homeschooled children to enjoy the extra benefits of peer interaction and involvement in sports or clubs.

7 Whatever the arguments for or against, homeschooling is a growing trend. There are now websites and support groups that help parents to assert their rights and enable them to learn more about educating their children. Once the last resort for troubled children, homeschooling is now embraced as an accepted alternative to the public educational system.

Verify Strategies

To build your reading fluency, it's important to be aware of how you use strategies to read, and to consider how successfully you are using them.

Use the questions in the Self Check on page 220 to think about your use of reading strategies.

Evaluate Progress

Evaluating your progress means thinking about how much you understood from the passage, and how fluently you were able to read the passage to get the information you needed.

Check how well you understood the passage by answering the following questions.

The author wrote this passage in order to _____ .
a   expose homeschooling as a threat to public education
b   show that homeschooling is superior to a public school education
c   discuss the growing trend of homeschooling
d   help parents cope with homeschooling their child

Up until about 200 years ago, there was no _____ .
a   education
b   homeschooling
c   community learning
d   public school system

In which country will parents find the most support for homeschooling?
a   England
b   Brazil
c   Spain
d   Germany

Which is NOT a problem mentioned in the passage regarding the public school system?
a   lack of teachers
b   lack of school activities
c   increased bullying
d   concern about their child's safety

Which is most likely to be true about homeschooled children?
a   They have more opportunities for social interaction.
b   They are better prepared for life outside the home.
c   They tend to get more attention from their teacher(s).
d   They don't do as well as school-educated children.

What is the main idea of paragraph 6?
a   Schools in the U.S. are trying to adapt to this growing trend of homeschooling.
b   Homeschooled children are still required to attend classes in school.
c   The U.S. government is trying to stop homeschooling.
d   Homeschooled children should get involved in sports and clubs.

What does the author mean when he says homeschooling was *once the last resort* in line 53?
a   It used to be mainly for children with learning difficulties.
b   It was finally accepted by various countries around the world.
c   It wasn't a priority for governments and schools.
d   It was the least attractive education option for many people.

SELF CHECK

A Here is a list of all the reading skills in *ACTIVE Skills for Reading Book 3*. For each skill, say whether you found the skill useful, not useful, or if you need more work with it. Check (✓) the box that applies.

Reading skill	Useful	Not useful	I need work
Arguing For and Against a Topic			
Identifying Cause and Effect			
Identifying Main and Supporting Ideas			
Identifying Main Ideas within Paragraphs			
Identifying Meaning from Context			
Making Inferences			
Predicting			
Previewing			
Recognizing Facts			
Recognizing Sequence of Events			
Scanning			
Skimming for the Main Idea			
Using Subheadings to Predict Content			

B Here are the four fluency strategies covered in the Review Units. For each strategy, say whether you found it useful, not useful, or if you need more work with it. Check (✓) the box that applies.

Fluency strategy	Useful	Not useful	I need work
Reading with a purpose: DRTA			
KWL			
SQ3R			
Reading ACTIVEly			

C Look again at the Are You an Active Reader? quiz on page 10 and complete your answers again. How has your reading fluency improved since you started this course?

Review Reading 7: You Can Be a World Memory Champion!

Fluency Practice

Time yourself as you read through the passage. Write down your time, then answer the questions on page 223. After answering the questions, correct your responses and write down your score. Record your performance on the Reading Rate Chart on page 240.

You Can Be a World Memory Champion!

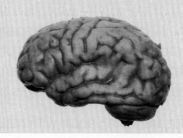

1 Every year, people with extraordinary memory skills compete in a unique event called the World Memory Championships. The tasks they are required to do require tremendous powers of memory retention: looking at and reciting a two-page poem; recollecting a page of 40-digit numbers; remembering the order of 52 cards in a deck; memorizing the names of 110 people
5 after looking at their pictures; and several other demanding tasks. Completing any of these tasks may not seem feasible for the average person, but scientific evidence seems to show that even someone with average skills can, through training, enhance his or her memory skills and be transformed into a memory champion.

2 One memory champion explained his
10 method of recalling the order of the cards in a deck. Previously, he linked a person, an action, and a thing to each card in the deck. For example, the king of hearts is Elvis Presley, eating, a peanut butter sandwich.
15 The three of spades is Rocky Balboa, boxing, Madison Square Garden. The ten of hearts is William Shakespeare, writing *Hamlet*, a broken pen. Take a person from the first card, an action from the second card, and
20 a thing from the third card. Then any group of three cards creates a vivid image that

a competitor trying hard to memorize cards as he takes part in the 21st World Memory Championships in December 2012

is more easily recalled. For example: king-ten-three becomes Elvis Presley writing *Hamlet* in Madison Square Garden—a memorable image.

3 25 Still, even having created images for each group of three cards, it is difficult to keep them in order. This is done using the *loci method*, or what some call a "Memory Palace" —a term created by Frances Yates in his 1966 book *The*
30 *Art of Memory* — which is a simple yet effective method devised by the ancient Greeks. They practised transforming lists of words into vivid

A competitor from China awaits instructions.

sets of objects, which they arranged in their imagination around familiar spaces. Then they learned to link these images back to their original meaning.

4 35 But are there people with naturally superior memories? We've all heard of people with photographic memories—the ability to memorize anything just by looking at it. Rajan Mahadevan, born in India in 1957, seemed to have such a memory. By the age of five, he was able to remember the license plate numbers of a parking lot full of cars. He was also able to remember a string of 31,811 digits. One book claimed that his memory power was a
40 natural talent. Later, however, Mahadevan visited with K. Anders Ericsson, a psychologist who believes that memory is a matter of training, not talent. They discussed Mahadevan's memory achievements, and Mahadevan explained that he had spent 1,000 hours and used memory techniques to memorize the 31,811 digits. He admitted that it was hard training that allowed him to do it, not a special memory.

5 45 The winner of the 2011 World Memory Championships, held in Guangzhou, China, was 21-year-old Chinese national Wang Feng. He retained his title from the previous year by breaking world records for three of the competition's ten memory games. These records were recalling 300 of 400 spoken numbers, and memorizing 500 numbers in five minutes and 2,660 numbers in one hour. But Wang Feng says he had a "normal memory as a child," and no
50 special talent except for hard work and attention to detail. "I've spent three months preparing for this championship," he said. "Each day I spend five to six hours practicing. Actually, each year, I spend two to three months preparing for competitions."

6 Although many still think that people have either good or bad memories from birth, that need not be true. By using the methods of grouping, linking to vivid images, and the loci method,
55 we can all enhance our memories. Who knows—you might even become the next World Memory Champion!

627 words   **Time taken** _____

Reading Comprehension

1 The author's purpose in writing is to _____ .
   a praise World Memory Champions
   b explain how only special people have great memories
   c give the history of the World Memory Championships
   d show how a good memory is more a matter of training than of talent

2 Which memory task is not mentioned in the passage?
   a remembering the order of a deck of cards
   b memorizing a poem
   c remembering a drawing
   d memorizing names

3 Based on the method in paragraph 2, which sequence of cards is represented by William Shakespeare eating at Madison Square Garden?
   a king-three-ten
   b three-king-ten
   c ten-king-three
   d ten-three-king

4 Why is the loci method useful for memorizing the order of a deck of cards?
   a It makes images even more vivid.
   b It assists with remembering the order of the three-card groups.
   c It allows landmarks to be more easily recalled.
   d It helps make things and places more familiar.

5 According to the passage, which is most likely true about Rajan Mahadevan?
   a His memory skill was a natural talent.
   b He was good at remembering things since childhood.
   c He had spent 1,000 hours learning memory techniques.
   d His powers of memory were actually a hoax.

6 According to the passage, what is true about Wang Feng?
   a He was born with excellent memory skills.
   b He does not need to prepare much for competitions.
   c 2011 was the first time he had won the championship.
   d He is very good at memorizing numbers.

7 What tone does the author take in the final paragraph?
   a negative
   b encouraging
   c neutral
   d cautious

Fluency Practice

Time yourself as you read through the passage. Write down your time, then answer the questions on page 226. After answering the questions, correct your responses and write down your score. Record your performance on the Reading Rate Chart on page 240.

MANGA, MANHWA, AND MANHUA

The concept of using pictures with words to tell a story has existed for thousands of years, since the ancient civilizations in Egypt and China. The first published comic book using speech balloons to show dialog is often reported to be *The Yellow Kid*, which debuted in 1896. The content of early comic books was nearly always humorous—

5 E. Segar's famous *Popeye* is one example. In the early 20th century, however, comic book plots became more diverse, with many hero and adventure stories. Many western comic books made their way to countries in Asia, where they inspired generations of cartoonists.

10 In the U.S. and many European countries, the best known type of East Asian comic book is probably Japanese *manga*. In the 1950s and 60s, the Japanese artist Osamu Tezuka produced a variety of manga for children, such as *Kimba the White Lion* and *Astro Boy*. His books often included

15 mature and tragic themes. By the 1980s and 90s, manga was no longer just for young children. It had conquered the teenage and young adult markets as well. In fact, by the late 20th century, manga represented 40 percent of all Japanese publishing.

Astroboy

20 The South Korean version of comic books or graphic novels is called *manhwa*. Much of early 20th century manhwa was used to speak out against oppression and injustice. Around the time of the Korean War in the 1950s, manhwa also provided a welcome es-cape for young people. Today, South Korea is a highly-developed
25 country and has some of the fastest Internet speeds in the world, so many people prefer to read manhwa (or translations of manga) online via computer or cell phone. Many popular Korean television dramas and movies have been based on manhwa. Over the last few years, interest in all things Korean has been on the rise around
30 the world, which has led to an increase in manhwa sales.

There is a long tradition of comic books in Chinese. The development of special printing techniques in the 19th century allowed the growth of *lianhuantu*—picture books which told a story. The modern term for comic books and graphic novels written in Chinese is *manhua*; some of them are original stories while others are translations from Japanese manga. As
35 in Korea, manhua have been used both for the expression of political opinions and as entertainment. Recently, a type of manhua genre called *wuxia* has become popular. These softcover or hardcover comics usually involve martial arts combat, like kungfu. The famous story *Crouching Tiger, Hidden Dragon* can be read as a wuxia comic. A well-drawn and well-written wuxia comic can provide a similar experience to an exciting martial arts movie.

40 Asian comics are a growing influence in western countries, where the market for them is increasing each year. The biggest consumer of manga outside of Japan is France. "In Europe, manga is most popular in France, then Italy and Spain," said Hyoe Narita, president of VIZ Media Europe, a Japanese entertainment company. About ten million manga books are sold in France annually. Japanese manga has had a strong influence on French
45 cartoonists, who try to combine Asian and European drawing techniques. A new "French manga" genre emerged, known as *La nouvelle manga* ("the new manga").

Manga, manhwa, and manhua have all made great progress in recent decades and their influence on how the West views comics is getting stronger. Thanks to the Internet and a number of small independent comic distributors, a growing number of fans outside Asia
50 can now follow and enjoy the latest manga, manhwa, and manhua.

592 words   **Time taken** _____

Reading Comprehension

1 What does the passage mainly discuss?
   a competition among East Asian comics
   b the future of East Asian comics in Europe
   c the influence of Western comics on East Asian comics
   d East Asian comic books and their relationship with the West

2 Which statement is true about early 20th century comic books?
   a They had a more diverse range of genres than today.
   b They were the first comic books.
   c They were nearly always humorous.
   d They didn't have speech balloons.

3 Which of the following is an example of Japanese manga?
   a The Yellow Kid
   b Popeye
   c Astro Boy
   d Manhwa

4 Which statement about manhwa is NOT true?
   a They were more popular in the 1950s.
   b They can be read on the Internet.
   c Television dramas have been based on them.
   d They have been used to speak out against injustice.

5 Which of the following is a Chinese martial arts comic?
   a lianhuantu
   b manhua
   c wuxia
   d manhwa

6 According to the passage, in which of these places is the most manga sold?
   a Korea
   b France
   c the United States
   d Hong Kong

7 In the final paragraph, what is the author's tone regarding the future of manga?
   a humorous
   b unfavorable
   c critical
   d optimistic

Vocabulary Glossary

Unit 1
Chapter 1

add up /æd ʌp/ *phr. v.* to become more and more: *If you're not careful, your problems will just add up.*

genuine /ˈʤɛnjʊɪn/ *adj.* sincere, honestly felt: *A salesman should have a genuine smile.*

navigate /ˈnævɪˌgeɪt/ *v.* to plan a path or direction, to find a way: *Paul used a map to navigate his way through the forest.*

personalize /ˈpɜːsənəˌlaɪz/ *v.* to make one's own; to make for oneself: *Students usually like to personalize their rooms on campus.*

potential /pəˈtɛnʃəl/ *adj.* possible: *We found a few potential customers at the conference.*

route /ruːt/ *n.* the way to get from one place to another: *The fastest route to the cabin is over the mountain.*

spare /spɛə/ *adj.* extra: *We keep a spare tire in the trunk of the car.*

treasure /ˈtrɛʒə/ *n.* something that is valued highly, a trophy: *The painting you found at the second-hand store is very rare.* It's a real treasure.

_____ _____

_____ _____

Chapter 2

abundant /əˈbʌndənt/ *adj.* in large quantities, more than enough: *Africa has abundant natural resources.*

convince /kənˈvɪns/ *v.* to make someone feel a certain idea is true: *Good salespeople can convince people to buy anything.*

facility /fəˈsɪləti/ *n.* rooms, equipment, or services provided for a particular purpose: *Most public parks have restroom facilities for anyone to use.*

lush /lʌʃ/ *adj.* looking healthy and strong, usually describing plants: *The Amazon rainforests are full of lush plants.*

palace /ˈpælɪs/ *n.* a home for someone royal, like a king or queen: *Kings and queens sometimes own several palaces.*

sanctuary /ˈsæŋktjʊərɪ/ *n.* a peaceful place that offers protection and a place to relax: *Animal sanctuaries protect many endangered species.*

shun /ʃʌn/ *v.* to ignore someone or something on purpose: *Some celebrities shun media attention.*

vast /vɑːst/ *adj.* extremely large: *The Sahara Desert is a vast area.*

_____ _____

_____ _____

Unit 2
Chapter 1

compile /kəmˈpaɪl/ *v.* to put information together into a logical order, especially so it can be analyzed: *Population censuses compile information on the residents of a country.*

convention /kənˈvɛnʃən/ *n.* a formal meeting for people with the same interests: *There are many comic book conventions around the world.*

data /ˈdɑːtə/ *n.* information or facts: *Computer hackers often try to access personal data.*

forecast /ˈfɔːrˌkæst/ *n.* a description of what is likely to happen in the future using information currently available: *Let's check the news channel to see the weather forecast for this weekend.*

intuition /ˌɪntuˈɪʃən/ *n.* the ability to understand or know something because of a feeling and not because of facts: *Dogs seem to have good intuition.*

optimistic /ˈɑptəˌmɪzəm/ *adj.* believing that good things will happen in the future: *Doctors say that being optimistic is good for your health.*

stick /stɪk/ *v.* to become permanent or lasting: *Many new trends come into fashion but don't stick.*

survey /sɜːˈveɪ/ *v.* to look at or think about something carefully, usually to make an opinion: *Let's survey the venue first before deciding whether to hold the concert there.*

_____   _____

_____   _____

Chapter 2

cautious /ˈkɔːʃəs/ *adj.* careful to avoid danger or risk: *Cautious people don't always succeed in business.*

collaborate /kəˈlæbəˌreɪt/ *v.* to work together as a group: *The best teams know how to collaborate to make a project work.*

episode /ˈɛpəˌsoʊd/ *n.* one part of a television or radio show series: *These days it's very easy to record an episode of your favorite show so you don't miss it.*

glamorous /ˈglæmərəs/ *adj.* attractive or exciting: *Movie stars often have very glamorous lifestyles.*

hesitate /ˈhɛzɪˌteɪt/ *v.* to pause before saying or doing something because you are nervous or not sure: *People who hesitate too much often don't get what they want.*

mislead /mɪsˈliːd/ *v.* to make someone believe something that is not true by giving them false or incomplete information: *The government has banned advertisements that deliberately try to mislead consumers.*

momentary /ˈmoʊmənˌtɛri/ *adj.* lasting for a very short time: *There was a momentary silence when we saw the beautiful view.*

pursue /pərˈsuː/ *v.* to continue doing an activity in order to achieve a goal: *If you want to pursue a career as a doctor you have to study hard.*

_____   _____

_____   _____

Unit 3
Chapter 1

critically /ˈkrɪtɪkəli/ *adv.* in a way that is very important: *Hospitals usually have units for critically ill people.*

culprit /ˈkʌlprɪt/ *n.* the reason for a particular problem or difficulty: *Bad decisions by banks were the main culprit behind recent economic problems.*

exploit /ˈɛksˌplɔɪt/ *v.* to treat someone unfairly by asking them to do things for you but not giving as much in return: *Big corporations have been accused of exploiting people in developing countries.*

imminent /ˈɪmənənt/ *adj.* likely to happen soon: *Some people believe that the end of the world is imminent.*

indefinitely /ɪnˈdɛfənɪtli/ *adv.* for a period of time that does not have a clear end point: *The sale will run indefinitely.*

intentional /ɪnˈtɛnʃənəl/ *adj.* done on purpose: *It is easier to forgive bad behavior if it isn't intentional.*

markedly /ˈmɑːrktli/ *adv.* in a way that is easy to notice: *American accents are markedly different from British accents.*

overwhelm /ˌoʊvərˈhwɛlm/ *v.* affect strongly so that a person cannot think clearly: *Travelers can be overwhelmed when they visit a country that is very different from their own.*

_____   _____

_____   _____

Chapter 2

conduct /kənˈdʌkt/ *v.* to carry out an activity to get information or prove facts: *To prove scientific theories, tests must be conducted.*

era /ˈɪrə/ *n.* a long period of time: *Art in the modern era is not the same as art in the old days.*

fitting /ˈfɪtɪŋ/ *adj.* right for a particular situation or occasion: *The statue of Charles Darwin at London's Natural History Museum is a fitting tribute.*

frail /freɪl/ *adj.* weak, not strong: *When people get older they become frail.*

inject /ɪnˈdʒɛkt/ *v.* to put a liquid inside a body using a device with a needle called a syringe: *In many countries, children are injected with vaccines when they are young.*

opposition /ˌɒpəˈzɪʃən/ *n.* strong disagreement with a plan or system: *Opposition to policies that damage the environment is natural.*

revive /rɪˈvaɪv/ *v.* to bring back to life: *First aid is vital if someone has to be revived after they have stopped breathing.*

worthwhile /ˈwɜrθˈhwaɪl/ *adj.* useful or important: *Volunteer work is always a worthwhile activity.*

_____   _____

_____   _____

Unit 4
Chapter 1

dense /dɛns/ *adj.* thick; close together: *Finding your way in dense forests can be tricky.*

fulfil /fʊlˈfɪl/ *v.* to achieve a stated goal or promise: *It is sad when a promising young musician quits before he fulfills his potential.*

in reality /ɪn riˈæləti/ *phr.* actually; in fact: *Ireland is often mistakenly said to be part of Britain, whereas, in reality, it is another country.*

inflation /ɪnˈfleɪʃən/ *n.* a continuing increase in prices over time: *When food prices go up, you can be sure inflation is occurring.*

investment /ɪnˈvɛstmənt/ *n.* something worth buying because it may be useful or worth more in the future: *Investments, like property and bars of gold, are a good way of saving for the future.*

necessity /nəˈsɛsəti/ *n.* something that you must have in order to live properly, e.g. food and housing: *In some countries, the poorest people cannot afford basic necessities.*

property /ˈprɒpərti/ *n.* things that one owns; often used to talk about one's house or land: *You should always protect your property as best you can.*

salary /ˈsæləri/ *n.* money one is paid for working: *Salaries have remained the same in my country for almost a decade.*

Chapter 2

affluent /ˈæfluənt/ *adj.* wealthy and having nice, expensive things: *Affluent people have fewer worries than people who struggle to make a living.*

ban /bæn/ *v.* to not allow: *Smoking in public places is banned in many countries.*

debt /dɛt/ *n.* money owed: *It is not a good idea to get into too much debt.*

extravagant /ɛkˈstrævəgənt/ *adj.* spending or costing more money than is reasonable: *People are generally more extravagant when they are young.*

sensible /ˈsɛnsəbəl/ *adj.* reasonable, practical, with good judgment: *Sensible people make good decisions.*

tricky /ˈtrɪki/ *adj.* difficult, complicated: *Preparing for an interview can be tricky.*

unforeseen /ʌnfɔːrˈsiːn/ *adj.* not expected: *Small events can have unforeseen consequences.*

wisely /ˈwaɪzli/ *adv.* in a smart way: *Parents always try to advise their children wisely.*

Unit 5
Chapter 1

afford /əˈfɔːrd/ *v.* to have enough money, be able to buy: *Most people can't afford to stay in luxury hotels all the time when they are on vacation.*

appropriate /əˈproupriət/ *adj.* right for the situation: *Make sure you wear appropriate footwear when hiking.*

customary /ˈkʌstəˌmeri/ *adj.* normal because the action is done in the usual or traditional way: *It is customary to give red envelopes during Chinese New Year.*

engrave /ɛnˈgreiv/ *v.* to mark, usually putting a name or a special message on an object: *Some couples engrave their wedding rings with their partner's initials.*

eternal /iˈtɜrnəl/ *adj.* never-ending: *A person might die, but their spirit is eternal.*

fabric /ˈfæbrɪk/ *n.* cloth: *Good clothes are made from high-quality fabric.*

integrate /ˈɪntəˌgreit/ *v.* to blend or combine things together so they are more effective: *Big cities such as New York integrate elements of many different cultures.*

vice versa /ˌvaɪs ˈvɜrsə/ *phr.* used to say the opposite of a situation just described is also true: *Opposition parties normally criticize governments and vice versa.*

_____   _____

_____   _____

Chapter 2

collide /kəˈlaɪd/ *v.* to smash together: *Some atoms form a chemical bond when they collide.*

drive away /draɪv əˈwei/ *phr. v.* to force to leave: *If you are always negative, you will drive all your friends away.*

explosion /ɛkˈsplouʒən/ *n.* a violent burst of energy: *Factories that use volatile chemicals are at risk of explosions.*

in return /ɪn rɪˈtɜrn/ *phr.* exchange for: *Show respect to others and they will show you respect in return.*

legend /ˈlɛdʒənd/ *n.* an old and traditional story: *Many stories that are accepted as history are actually legends.*

nevertheless /ˌnɛvərðəˈlɛs/ *adv.* in contrast to: *Starting your own business is difficult; nevertheless, it can be rewarding.*

stuff /stʌf/ *v.* to put something inside another thing: *Green peppers can be stuffed with cheese to make a tasty meal.*

worship /ˈwɜrʃɪp/ *v.* to show respect to a god, for example, by praying: *People who follow Hinduism worship many different gods and goddesses.*

_____   _____

_____   _____

Unit 6
Chapter 1

altitude /ˈæltəˌtuːd/ *n.* the height of an object or place above the sea: *High altitudes can cause sickness.*

baffle /ˈbæfəl/ *v.* to not understand or be able to explain: *Some problems of science baffle even the most intelligent people.*

fictional /ˈfɪkʃənəl/ *adj.* imaginary or from a book or story: *Writers can choose to set their novels in fictional locations.*

inaccessible /ˌɪnækˈsɛsəbəl/ *adj.* difficult or impossible to reach: *Parts of rainforests in Africa are almost inaccessible.*

remote /rɪˈmoʊt/ *adj.* far away, isolated: *Even the world's most remote locations now have Internet access.*

speculate /ˈspɛkjəˌleɪt/ *v.* to guess about the cause or effect of something without knowing all the details: *For centuries, people have speculated about the origin of the universe.*

summit /ˈsʌmɪt/ *n.* the highest level of something, such as a mountain: *It takes days to reach the summit of the world's highest mountains.*

terrain /təˈreɪn/ *n.* land, usually preceded by an adjective: *Taiwan has some really challenging terrain for cyclists.*

_____   _____

_____   _____

Chapter 2

external /ɛkˈstɪriər/ *adj.* on the outside of a surface or body: *Businesses are affected by many external factors such as economic conditions and government policy.*

function /ˈfʌŋkʃən/ *v.* to work in the correct or intended way: *If a system is functioning well, there is no need to change it.*

scenario /səˈnɛriˌoʊ/ *n.* a situation that could possibly happen: *To prepare for unexpected situations, it's best to imagine different scenarios.*

spontaneous /spɒnˈteɪniəs/ *adj.* done without plan or as a surprise: *The best speakers prepare before an event, but they can also be spontaneous.*

supposedly /səˈpoʊzɪdli/ *adv.* when something is believed to be true by many people: *Paul's band is supposedly pretty good, but I've never heard them.*

thorough /ˈθəroʊ/ *adj.* complete, examined with a lot of effort: *Thorough research into climate change is required.*

ventilate /ˈvɛntəˌleɪt/ *v.* to allow fresh air to come into a space: *You should keep the windows open to ventilate a room properly.*

victim /ˈvɪktəm/ *n.* a person who is hurt in a situation: *Victims of violent crime can have trouble getting over the experience.*

_____   _____

_____   _____

Unit 7

Chapter 1

alternate /ˈɔːltəˌneɪt/ *v.* to change or occur in turn repeatedly: *To maintain your focus at work, it helps to alternate the kinds of tasks you are doing.*

fad /fæd/ *n.* something people like or do for a short period of time: *Fads come and go with different generations.*

fed up with /fɛd ʌp wɪð/ *phr. v.* to become upset or annoyed, and wanting a situation to change: *If you are fed up with your job, perhaps it is time for a career change.*

go overboard /goʊ ˈoʊvərˌbɔːrd/ *phr.* to do too much: *Working hard is important, but you shouldn't go overboard.*

loaded with /ˈloʊdɪd wɪð/ *phr. v.* completely full: *Great poetry is loaded with imagery.*

portion /ˈpɔːʃən/ *n.* an amount of food for one person: *Reducing the size of your meal portions can help you lose weight.*

struggle /ˈstrʌgəl/ *n.* a difficult challenge: *It can be a struggle to stay motivated in a job you don't like.*

veteran /ˈvɛtərən/ *n.* someone who has a lot of experience in a particular activity: *Veterans in any industry can offer their experience to the younger generation.*

_____   _____

_____   _____

Chapter 2

absorb /əbˈsɔːb/ *v.* to reduce the effect of a sudden (violent) movement: *Boxers move their heads backwards to absorb the shock of punches.*

ache /eɪk/ *n.* a continuous, but not sharp, pain: *As you get older, aches and pains become more common.*

adapt /əˈdæpt/ *v.* to gradually change to make suitable for a different purpose: *Many great novels have been adapted for TV and film.*

balance /ˈbæləns/ *n.* to keep weight evenly spread out so you do not fall: *Balancing on a surfboard is not easy for beginners.*

clear-cut /klɪə kʌt/ *adj.* easy to understand or be certain about, definite: *We all need clear-cut goals in life.*

gain /geɪn/ *v.* to get or increase: *The more you practice a skill, the more you gain confidence.*

persistent /pəˈsɪstənt/ *adj.* continuing to happen longer than usual or desired: *Malaria is a persistent problem in developing countries.*

rush /rʌʃ/ *v.* to do something too quickly and without enough time to do it carefully or well: *Don't rush your homework or you might make mistakes.*

_____   _____

_____   _____

Unit 8
Chapter 1

confine /kən'faɪn/ *v.* keep within a certain limit: *It's best to confine your comments to the topic in hand at office meetings.*

distribute /dɪ'strɪbjuːt/ *v.* to share things within a group: *Charities distribute food and clothing to the poor during the Christmas period.*

duration /djʊ'reɪʃən/ *n.* the length of time that something continues: *When you're in a movie theater, you should be quiet for the duration of the film.*

expedition /ˌekspɪ'dɪʃən/ *n.* a long and carefully organized journey to a dangerous or unfamiliar place: *Roald Amundsen led the first successful expedition to the South Pole.*

exposed /ɪk'spoʊzd/ *v.* to have contact with something, either by seeing, smelling, or breathing: *Walking around most parks in spring, you're exposed to the smell of flowers and sounds of birds.*

intense /ɪn'tens/ *adj.* having a very strong effect or felt very strongly: *Politicians are always under intense pressure to fulfill their promises.*

mission /'mɪʃən/ *n.* an important job or task: *A new rover mission to Mars will take place in 2020.*

sacrifice /'sækrɪˌfaɪs/ *n.* act of not doing something in order to do something more important: *We all have to make sacrifices in our lives.*

_____   _____

_____   _____

Chapter 2

behind schedule /bɪ'haɪnd 'ʃedjuːl/ *phr.* late: *If you find you're always behind schedule, perhaps you need to plan better.*

devise /dɪ'vaɪz/ *v.* to plan or invent a new way of doing something: *Scientists are devising new green technologies as we speak.*

far-fetched /fɑː fetʃd/ *adj.* very unlikely to be true or to happen: *People who tell far-fetched tales are seldom believed.*

innovation /ˌɪnə'veɪʃən/ *n.* a new idea, method, or invention: *London is famous for its innovations in the design sector.*

primitive /'prɪmɪtɪv/ *adj.* simple, without modern features that make it better or faster: *Primitive humans lived in caves.*

principle /'prɪnsɪpəl/ *n.* a moral rule or believe about what is right or wrong: *Always stay true to your principles.*

steer /stɪər/ *v.* to guide or control: *Belief in yourself will help steer you through tough times.*

witness /'wɪtnɪs/ *v.* to see something like a crime or accident happen: *If you witness a crime, you should report it to the police.*

_____   _____

_____   _____

Unit 9
Chapter 1

advocate /ˈædvəkɪt/ *n.* a person who publicly supports a person, idea, or thing: *Most economists these days are advocates of free trade.*

circumstance /ˈsɜːkəmstəns/ *n.* the conditions that affect a situation, action, or event: *No matter the circumstances, you should treat others as you expect to be treated.*

content /kənˈtɛnt/ *adj.* happy and satisfied: *You should never be content to accept a bad deal.*

dilemma /dɪˈlɛmə/ *n.* a situation that is difficult to decide what to do in because all choices seem equally good or bad: *Life is full of dilemmas.*

negotiate /nɪˈgoʊʃɪˌeɪt/ *v.* to discuss something in order to reach an agreement: *In any business deal, the parties involved have to negotiate.*

self-esteem /sɛlf-ɪˈstiːm/ *n.* the feeling of being satisfied with your own abilities: *Self-esteem is an important part of happiness.*

sibling /ˈsɪblɪŋ/ *n.* a brother or sister: *A person who doesn't have any siblings is called an only child.*

stigma /ˈstɪgmə/ *n.* a strong feeling in society against a particular illness or something to be ashamed of: *In some societies there is a stigma against single mothers.*

_____   _____

_____   _____

Chapter 2

absent /æbˈsɛnt/ *adj.* not at a place because you are sick or decide not to go: *If you're absent from work, you might need to have a doctor's note.*

hang out /hæŋ aʊt/ *phr. v.* spend a lot of time in a particular place or with particular people: *Kids like to hang out with people with similar interests.*

intention /ɪnˈtɛnʃən/ *n.* a plan or desire to do something: *Good intentions don't always lead to action.*

presence /ˈprɛzəns/ *n.* when someone or something is present in a particular place: *The presence of CO_2 in the atmosphere is thought to be causing global warming.*

priority /praɪˈɒrɪtɪ/ *n.* something that is important and needing attention before anything else: *Getting one's priorities in order is not easy.*

sole /soʊl/ *adj.* the only one: *China is Asia's sole representative on the United Nations Security Council.*

thereby /ˌðɛəˈbaɪ/ *adv.* with the result that something else happens: *Many businesses use tax avoidance laws, thereby damaging their country's economy.*

transition /trænˈzɪʃən/ *n.* when something changes from one form or state to another: *The best kind of writing uses clear transitions to move from one idea to another.*

_____   _____

_____   _____

Unit 10
Chapter 1

distract /dɪˈstrækt/ *v.* to draw attention away from one's focus: *He has to study in the library because he is easily distracted by noise.*

entail /ɪnˈteɪl/ *v.* to involve or include: *Being a good athlete entails a high level of fitness.*

erratic /ɪˈrætɪk/ *adj.* inconsistent; irregular; without a set schedule or pattern: *Her behavior has been erratic lately; she's happy one minute and sad the next.*

pace /peɪs/ *n.* speed; rate of progress: *We could work at a quicker pace if everyone cooperates.*

perspective /pəˈspɛktɪv/ *n.* point of view; the place from which one sees something: *We all have different perspectives on life.*

prestigious /prɛˈstɪʤəs/ *adj.* having a very good reputation: *The Oscars are considered the most prestigious awards show in the film industry.*

reliable /rɪˈlaɪəbəl/ *adj.* dependable: *Laptops are not considered as reliable as desktop computers.*

supplement /ˈsʌplɪˌmɛnt/ *v.* to complete or make an addition: *Vegetarians should supplement their diets with vitamins.*

_____   _____

_____   _____

Chapter 2

akin to /əˈkɪn tuː/ *adj.* very similar to something: *Some fashions these days are akin to styles from the past.*

automatically /ˌɔːtəˈmætɪkli/ *adv.* independently, or unconsciously: *In an automatic car, the gears change automatically as speed increases or decreases*

cheat /ʧiːt/ *v.* to behave in a dishonest way to win or have an advantage: *Cheating on a test is not a good idea.*

cite /saɪt/ *v.* to mention something as an example that supports or proves an idea or situation: *When writing academic papers, students need to cite all their sources.*

clarity /ˈklærɪtɪ/ *n.* the state of being clear and easy to understand: *Expressing oneself with clarity is not easy.*

draft /drɑːft/ *n.* a piece of writing or plan that is not in its finished form: *Before submitting an important report, you should have someone read the final draft.*

offense /ˈɒfɛns/ *n.* something that is done wrong and against the rules: *Driving offenses carry penalties in most countries.*

well-meaning /wɛl ˈmiːnɪŋ/ *adj.* intending to be helpful: *Even well-meaning people can be misunderstood.*

_____   _____

_____   _____

Unit 11
Chapter 1

classify /ˈklæsɪˌfaɪ/ *v.* to put things into groups: *Different types of music are not always easy to classify.*

complication /ˌkɒmplɪˈkeɪʃən/ *n.* a problem that happens after another situation and makes it more difficult: *Signing a contract avoids complications and misunderstandings.*

consciously /ˈkɒnʃəslɪ/ *adv.* in a knowing way, awake and aware: *Some people are consciously rude while others do not realize they are not being nice.*

no matter /noʊ ˈmætə/ *phr.* used to say something is true whatever the situation is: *No matter how hard you try, you can never satisfy some people.*

reflection /rɪˈflɛkʃən/ *n.* an image that you can see in a mirror, glass, or water: *Reflections in a mirror look different depending on your angle.*

reverse /rɪˈvɜːs/ *adj.* the opposite direction or order than before: *Scolding him will have the reverse effect of making him not want to do household chores.*

strikingly /ˈstraɪkɪŋlɪ/ *adv.* in a way that is easy to notice: *Famous models are strikingly beautiful.*

trace /treɪs/ *v.* to find the origins of something: *The origins of the modern computer can be traced to the 19th century.*

_____   _____

_____   _____

Chapter 2

accelerate /ækˈsɛləˌreɪt/ *v.* to gain speed: *The Internet has helped accelerate learning in many ways.*

feasible /ˈfiːzəbəl/ *adj.* able to be made, done, or achieved: *Some good plans are not always feasible.*

guarantee /ˌgærənˈtiː/ *n.* something that makes certain that something else will happen, or is true: *A famous brand name is not always a guarantee of good quality.*

landmark /ˈlændˌmɑːk/ *n.* a significant or outstanding feature in an area: *The Eiffel Tower is France's most famous landmark.*

recollect /ˌrɛkəˈlɛkt/ *v.* to remember: *Old people often recollect their childhoods in detail.*

tremendous /trɪˈmɛndəs/ *adj.* very great in amount or level: *A tremendous amount of work goes into writing a book.*

visualize /ˈvɪʒʊəˌlaɪz/ *v.* to form a picture in your mind: *Visualizing a world with no war is not easy.*

vivid /ˈvɪvɪd/ *adj.* bright, colorful, or intense: *A great writer can create vivid pictures in a reader's head.*

_____   _____

_____   _____

Unit 12
Chapter 1

compelling /kəmˈpɛlɪŋ/ *adj.* having a powerful effect, requiring attention and respect: *There is no compelling argument for the existence of ghosts.*

conflict /kənˈflɪkt/ *v.* when two ideas or opinions exist but cannot both be true: *The beliefs of some groups always conflict with others'.*

embrace /ɪmˈbreɪs/ *v.* to fully accept an idea or opinion: *Nations that embrace new technology always thrive.*

emerge /ɪˈmɜːʤ/ *v.* to appear or come out of somewhere: *As rainforests have been cut down, several tribes have emerged from the jungle.*

endure /ɪnˈdjʊə/ *v.* to remain or continue to exist for a long time: *Great works of art endure through the ages.*

invincible /ɪnˈvɪnsəbəl/ *adj.* too strong to be destroyed or defeated: *Despite what people think, no human is invincible.*

patriotic /ˌpeɪtrɪˈɒtɪk/ *adj.* having or expressing a great love for your country: *Seeing a country's flag or hearing a national anthem usually makes people feel very patriotic.*

subsequently /ˈsʌbsɪkwəntli/ *adv.* afterwards; later: *The book was written five years ago and has subsequently been translated into several languages.*

_____   _____

_____   _____

Chapter 2

convey /kənˈveɪ/ *v.* to communicate or express something with or without words: *It's not always easy to convey ideas when communicating with text messages.*

deviate /ˈdiːvɪˌeɪt/ *v.* to change away from the original plan: *Try not to deviate from the topic too much when giving a speech.*

intricate /ˈɪntrɪkɪt/ *adj.* containing many small parts or details that all work or fit together: *Good city maps provide intricate detail of different districts.*

mainstream /ˈmeɪnˌstriːm/ *adj.* involving most people in society: *Mainstream opinion is not always correct.*

pull off /pʊl ɒf/ *phr. v.* to successfully execute an action: *Several painters have pulled off forgeries of well-known works.*

retain /rɪˈteɪn/ *v.* to keep or continue to have something: *New versions of software tend to retain features from the old versions.*

sequel /ˈsiːkwəl/ *n.* a book, movie, etc that continues a story of an earlier one: *Movie sequels are frequently not as good as the first part.*

unrelenting /ˌʌnrɪˈlɛntɪŋ/ *adj.* continued in a determined way without thinking about anyone else's feelings: *Effective journalists must be unrelenting when looking for the truth.*

_____   _____

_____   _____

Prefixes, Roots and Suffixes

Here is a list of prefixes, roots, and suffixes that appear in this book.

Prefixes
con, com with or together: *connection, communicate*; **cross-** across: *cross-country, cross-cultural*; **de, dis, div** not, negative: *deduct, disapprove, disgrace*; **fore** before: *forecast, foreword*; **em/en** (to put) into or to cover: *empower, enhance*; **ex** upwards, completely, without, or former: *exhausting, experience, exclusive*; **im, in, il, ir** not, negative: *impossible, insecure, illiterate*; **im, in, ir** related to inside or inwards: *inflation, inspect, irrigate*; **inter** between two or more places or groups: *Internet, international*; **intro** within: *introduce*; **kilo** a thousand: *kilogram, kilometer*; **micro** very small: *microphone*; **milli** related to thousand: *million, milliliter, millimeter*; **mis** badly or wrongly: *miserable, mislead, misguided*; **off-** away from, out of, not on: *off-season, off-site*; **over** more: *overestimate, overpay*; **pre** done before or in advance: *precaution, predict, prepaid*; **re** again or back: *return, recall, retrieve*; **retro** coming back, from the past: *retroactive, retrograde*; **sub** below or under: *submit*; **tele** far: *television, telephone*; **trans** across: *transportation, transform*; **un** not, negative: *unaware, unethical, unidentified, unthinkable*; **under** less: *underway, underweight*; **uni** one: *university, united*; **well-** done well or a lot: *well-known, well-liked*

Root Words
bio related to life: *biology, biography*; **dic, dict** say, tell, speak: *dictate, dictionary*; **fic, fice** to do or to make, related to the suffix *-fy*: *beneficial, sufficient, magnify*; **geo** related to the earth: *geographic, geology*; **phon** related to the sound: *phonics*; **physio** nature/body: *physiology*; **psych** related to the mind: *psychologist*; **pub** related to people: *publicity, public*; **socio** related to the culture: *sociology*; **spec, spect** to observe or to watch: *speculation, inspect*; **vit, viv** life: *vitamin, vivid*

Suffixes
able full of: *beatable, believable*; **al** used to make an adjective from a noun: *additional, personal, national, vital*; **an, ian** relating to: *American, Australian, Italian*; **ant, ent** indicating an adjective: *extravagant, affluent*; **ate** used to make a verb from a noun: *associate, decorate, originate*; **ation, ution, ition** used to make a noun from a verb: *combination, resolution, competition*; **dom** state of being: *freedom, kingdom*; **eer** one who does something: *pioneer, volunteer*; **en** used to form verbs meaning to increase a quality: *harden, threaten, frighten*; **ence** added to some adjectives to make a noun: *confidence, excellence*; **ent** one who does something: *parent, student*; **er/or** someone or something that does something: *advertiser, competitor, reporter*; **er** (after an adjective) more: *faster, safer*; **est** (after an adjective) most: *safest*; **ful** filled with: *careful, powerful*; **hood** state of: *childhood, neighborhood*; **ion, sion, tion** indicating a noun: *admiration, competition*; **ine** indicating a verb: *combine*; **ish** relating to: *English, distinguish, Jewish*; **ism** an act of or process, state or condition: *plagiarism, patriotism*; **ist** one who does something: *artist, psychologist, tourist*; **ity** used to make a noun from an adjective: *charity, identity*; **ive** indicating an adjective: *aggressive, negative*; **ize, ise** to make or cause to become: *fertilize, surprise*; **less** without, not having: *hopeless, restless*; **logy, ology** the study of: *geology, technology*; **ly** used to form an adverb from an adjective: *especially, quickly*; **mate** companion: *roommate, classmate*; **ment** used to make a noun from a verb: *improvement, measurement, government*; **ness** used to make a noun from an adjective: *awareness, business, friendliness*; **ous, ious** relating to: *adventurous, curious, various*; **some** full of: *awesome, handsome*; **th** indicating an order: *eighteenth, sixth*; **ure** indicating some nouns: *culture, temperature, candidature*; **y** indicating an adjective: *flashy, healthy*

Reading Fluency Chart

Use this graph to record your progress for each of the eight Review Reading passages. Find the intersection of your reading rate and your comprehension score. Write the number of the review reading on the chart. Your goal is to be in Quadrant 4.

400	**Quadrant 2**					**Quadrant 4**	
380							
360							
340							
320							
300							
280							
260							
240							
220							
200							
180							
160							
140							
120							
100							
80							
60							
40	**Quadrant 1**					**Quadrant 3**	
	1 (14%)	2 (29%)	3 (43%)	4 (57%)	5 (71%)	6 (86%)	7 (100%)

Calculating your words-per-minute (wpm) At the end of each Review Reading passage you see the number of words in the passage (i.e. Review Reading #1 = 627 words). Divide your time into the number of words in the passage to get your wpm. For example, if you read Review Reading #1 in 3 minutes, your wpm equals 209 wpm (627/3 = 209).

Quadrant 1: You are reading slower than 200 wpm with less than 70% comprehension.
Quadrant 2: You are reading faster than 200 wpm with less than 70% comprehension.
Quadrant 3: You are reading slower than 200 wpm with greater than 70% comprehension.
Quadrant 4: You are reading faster than 200 wpm with greater than 70% comprehension.